VOLVO AILSA

Stewart J. Brown

Ian Allan
PUBLISHING

Contents

First published 2011

ISBN 978 0 7110 3514 0

Published by Ian Allan Publishing

an imprint of Ian Allan Publishing Ltd, Hersham, Surrey, KT12 4RG

Printed in England by Ian Allan Printing Ltd, Hersham, Surrey, KT12 4RG

Code: 1101/B

Distributed in the United States of America and Canada by BookMasters Distribution Services

Visit the Ian Allan Publishing website at www.ianallanpublishing.com

MIX
Paper from
responsible sources
FSC® C014615
FSC
www.fsc.org

Foreword

It's difficult to imagine a world in which one manufacturing group supplied all of Britain's double-deck buses, but that's how it was in the early 1970s, Bristol, Daimler and Leyland all being tied in to the British Leyland Motor Corporation. So when an importer of Scandinavian trucks took an interest in the British market, and with an unconventional model, nobody knew quite what to make of it. There were doubts about using a small turbocharged engine to power an urban double-deck bus, and questions about the wisdom of putting it at the front. But when it appeared, the Ailsa proved to be an eminently practical bus. Yes, for passengers it was noisier than rear-engined models, but it was on the whole reliable, and with no engine taking up space at the rear of the lower saloon it could accommodate an extra row of seats.

Just over 1,000 Ailsas — a respectable enough figure — were built over a 12-year period, almost a third being exported. Yet that masks what must have been a bit of a disappointment for its makers. The Scottish Bus Group, which supported the concept, bought fewer than 200 and continued to buy the very Fleetlines whose reliability it had cited as a reason for wanting a simpler bus with a front-mounted engine. In England the Ailsa achieved just over 160 sales, and its two biggest orders, from the West Midlands and South Yorkshire PTEs, were secured primarily because of British Leyland's inability to supply new buses quickly enough.

In Hong Kong, where operators shared SBG's concerns about the reliability of Fleetlines, just 10 Ailsas were sold — although orders for 320 from Indonesia were a worthwhile prize. But in the end the Scottish-built Ailsa turned out to be a Scottish bus. Of 716 Ailsas for UK fleets, 516 went to Scottish operators.

The Citybus, which replaced the Ailsa, was a different type of bus. The use of an underfloor engine set it apart from its competitors — and saw Leyland hastily develop a Citybus lookalike.

The Citybus found a much broader range of buyers, including many former Leyland customers. And despite its high floor the Citybus achieved considerable success in London, where just over 170 were bought between 1988 and 1991 for operation on London Regional Transport tendered services. Outside London the biggest users were Strathclyde PTE and Nottingham City Transport.

Despite wider acceptance of the Citybus, UK sales, at 586, were lower than those of the Ailsa, largely because of a dramatic decline in sales of big buses in the aftermath of deregulation and privatisation.

In preparing this volume I should like to acknowledge the kind assistance of Eric Hutchison and Neil Townend, and of two of the major figures involved with both models. One was Alan Westwell, who bought Ailsas when he was at Greater Glasgow PTE and Tayside, and then, on his return to Glasgow as Director General of Strathclyde PTE, bought 123 Ailsas and 101 Citybuses between 1981 and 1990; indeed, if you consider Alan Westwell's influence in Glasgow and at Tayside he was directly or indirectly involved in the purchase of 313 Ailsas, or 44% of all Ailsas delivered to British fleets. The other was Sandy Glennie, who for most of the period covered in this book was Managing Director of Volvo's British bus business.

The whine of the Ailsa has long since vanished from Britain's streets, but as this is being written there are still numbers of Citybuses about, typically around 20 years old, and a tribute to the reliability of the B10M chassis on which they were based.

Stewart J. Brown
Hebden Bridge
December 2010

The quest for reliability

The first production rear-engined double-deckers, Leyland Atlanteans, entered service in 1958. Yet 15 years later there were still bus fleet engineers who hankered after the simplicity and reliability of buses with the engine at the front and the straightforward drivetrain layout that went with it. The Atlantean — and the Daimler Fleetline which followed it — offered greater carrying capacity than the previous generation of front-engined double-deckers whose development could be traced back to the trend-setting Leyland Titan TD1 of 1927. They also allowed the driver to supervise passengers as they were boarding and alighting, which was perceived as improving safety when compared with an open-platform rear-entrance model. And ultimately they would allow operators to dispense with the services of a conductor, offering substantial cost savings — although that was not envisaged when the new models were unveiled.

Laudable as these features were, what early Atlanteans and Fleetlines did not offer was reliability. The Scottish Bus Group was particularly unhappy with the performance of its rear-engined Daimler Fleetlines and with the Bristol VRTs which followed. And that was the genesis of the Ailsa. Early promotional material used the line 'Remember the good old days when passengers kept coming — and buses kept going?' and added: 'British concept puts the clock back and the engine forward.'

It's easy to poke fun at conservative engineers who were slow to adapt to the new order, in which buses were more complex and therefore required more maintenance. But it's possible to sympathise with them too. The front-engined chassis that were being built for double-deck operation in the 1960s were, on the whole, supremely reliable. They were fuel-efficient and easy to maintain. A fleet engineer in the mid-1960s with a depot full of Leyland Titans or Bristol Lodekkas knew that with proper maintenance they would all leave the depot in the morning and all come back home again at night. Failures on the road were few and far between. And that's how it was at the Scottish Bus Group.

Reliable front-engined models were the backbone of the Scottish Bus Group's double-deck fleet until the mid-1960s. With the Ailsa SBG was hoping to return to the standards of reliability achieved by models such as the Bristol Lodekka. An Eastern Scottish FS6G leaves Edinburgh for Glasgow in 1978. The bus may be 15 years old, but it is still dependable — and for that reason perhaps a better bet for a long-distance service than the company's newer Fleetlines. Stewart J. Brown

The model which came to epitomise the Scottish Bus Group's dislike of rear-engined buses was the Bristol VRT. A Western SMT example operates a local service in Paisley in November 1972, but although only three years old its days are numbered and it will soon be heading south to join an NBC fleet in exchange for a Lodekka. That the VRTs enjoyed a normal operating life with NBC suggests problems with them while operating in Scotland may not have been entirely Bristol's fault.
Stewart J. Brown

SBG started buying Daimler Fleetlines in large numbers from 1965 and then Bristol VRTs from 1968. It was a measure of the VRT's unpopularity at SBG that all 109 bought between 1968 and 1970 had gone by 1974, and that some operated in Scotland for only 18 months. Seldom in the annals of bus history — except in London — has a major operator expressed so clearly its dissatisfaction with what it perceived as a troublesome vehicle.

SBG was none too happy with its Fleetlines either, and those bought by Central SMT lasted just four years before being transferred to other Group companies. Yet, despite all its complaints, during the years when both Fleetlines and Ailsas were available SBG did in fact buy more Fleetlines than Ailsas. A Post Office BMC LD van adds period colour to this view in Clyde Street, Glasgow, in 1973.
Stewart J. Brown

SBG persevered with the Fleetline, but after buying just over 400 by 1971 it started ordering increasing numbers of high-capacity single-deckers in the shape of 53-seat Alexander-bodied Leyland Leopards which were licensed to carry up to 24 standees. Never mind the three-step entrance; the Leopard was a reliable and economical workhorse. One SBG company, Central SMT, had 35 Fleetlines which it transferred elsewhere in the group when they were just four years old, deciding that the Leopard was a better bet. Central's management was of the opinion that service reliability was more important than easy passenger access.

In the early 1970s SBG voiced its concerns in its annual reports. The 1971 report noted that rear-engined double-deckers were 'still subject to an unduly high rate of mechanical failure', adding: 'Until the Group can obtain dependable double-deckers, intake is being confined to a minimum.' In its 1972 report it referred to 'a high degree of unreliability' and 'the increased rate of failure of certain components on newer vehicles, as compared with older vehicles which are much simpler in design'.

By 1973, as well as bemoaning the reliability of existing buses, SBG was 'awaiting with interest' the development of the Ailsa, commenting: 'If this vehicle can solve the double-deck problem, it will be welcomed.'

The Ailsa was intended to be the bus which would address all the ills associated with the Fleetline and the VRT. It was developed by a new company, Ailsa Bus, set up in 1971 by Ailsa Trucks, the Scottish-based importer of Volvo

trucks. The company had started importing trucks from Sweden in 1967 and had been phenomenally successful, achieving 2,000 sales a year by 1972.

The idea of a front-engined bus with the entrance in the front overhang alongside the driver had been tried before. In 1958 Guy unveiled its Wulfrunian, which used a Gardner 6LX engine. The sheer bulk of the engine made for a cramped driver's compartment and also compromised the entrance area — particularly when compared with the contemporary Leyland Atlantean, with its spacious and open area for both driver and passengers. There were many problems with the Wulfrunian — notably in its novel use of air suspension and disc brakes and the weight of the 10.45-litre engine located ahead of the front axle.

The designers at Ailsa were careful not to fall into any of the traps which some 15 years earlier had sunk the Wulfrunian — and helped sink Guy with it. For a start they used a 6.7-litre Volvo TD70 engine, which was compact, powerful and lighter than a 6LX (or any other contemporary bus engine). It was, indeed, the smallest engine ever fitted to a production double-deck bus in Britain. The engine was turbocharged, which was unusual for an urban bus at this time, and the turbocharger contributed to the Ailsa's distinctive 'whistle' while on the move. It used a Self-Changing Gears Pneumocyclic gearbox — SCG was part of the Leyland organisation but was free to sell its gearboxes to other manufacturers — and this was mounted in mid-wheelbase to improve weight distribution. Other features to

The Guy Wulfrunian used the same general layout as the Ailsa but with a Gardner engine, a low frame and advanced features such as independent front suspension and disc brakes. Most were bodied by Roe. One of Guy's demonstrators was evaluated by Western SMT in Kilmarnock in 1961; 17 years later Western would operate Ailsas.
Gavin Booth collection

aid weight distribution were the location of the fuel tank and the batteries at the rear of the chassis. Leaf suspension was fitted; this was still standard practice on most British buses. The Leyland National, launched in 1972, marked the first successful commercial application of air suspension to a British urban bus.

Apart from the engine location, the most interesting thing about the Ailsa was the design of its chassis. Instead of a conventional ladder frame — the accepted chassis layout since the dawn of the bus industry — the Ailsa had a perimeter frame which was cranked up over the front and rear wheels. A similar layout had been developed by Bristol for the F-series Lodekka (and would be used in 1980 by Leyland for its Olympian). There was a central spine, on top of which lay the cross-members running transversely between the outer frame. This chassis layout was more rigid than the ladder frame used on rear-engined models, which had a tendency to flex because of the weight of the engine behind the rear axle. The model was given the Volvo type code AB57, later changed to B55.

Much of the development work on the Ailsa was done in conjunction with bodybuilder Alexander, a logical choice in that the Falkirk-based company supplied the bulk of SBG's bodywork. The AV-style body which was developed for the Ailsa was clearly related to the new aluminium-framed AL-style body, introduced in 1972 and fitted to Atlantean, Fleetline and ultimately also to VRT chassis. The chassis had a 16ft 3in (4.95m) wheelbase, and when bodied by Alexander the complete vehicle was 32ft 4in (9.85m) long.

In 1972 Volvo purchased a 75% stake in the Ailsa Truck and Ailsa Bus businesses, and in readiness for vehicle assembly a site, formerly occupied by a Royal Ordnance factory, was acquired on the edge of Irvine. The business would become a wholly owned Volvo subsidiary in 1975.

The first completed Ailsa had chassis number 73/1 — year 1973, chassis No 1 — and was exhibited at the Scottish Motor Show at Glasgow's Kelvin Hall in November 1973, in the livery of Alexander Midland. Ailsa's launch statement described the vehicle as 'a completely new double-deck bus, conceived, designed and built in Scotland utilising 95% British components'. Britishness was an issue for public-sector bus buyers in the 1970s.

The body featured a three-leaf entrance door, which folded open towards the front of the bus, eliminating the obstruction of the area to the right of the entrance which would have been caused by the rear section of a conventional four-leaf door. The two-step entrance was described by Ailsa as a 'clear low entry', which by

The Wulfrunian had a nearside staircase and a narrow gangway between the front wheels. It also had a step-free entrance. Where bodybuilders on the Ailsa used a three-leaf entrance door, which folded forwards, for the Wulfrunian Roe used a four-leaf double-jack-knife but with narrow leaves on the rear section and wide leaves on the front. This made for easier access to the stairs. Gavin Booth collection

the standards of 1973 it was. There was a forward-ascending staircase, which meant there were no seats on the offside at the front of the upper deck, the layout reducing the load on the front axle. The bus seated 79 passengers (44 upstairs, 35 down) — four more than on a standard SBG Fleetline; the absence of an

Ailsa's official picture of the first chassis shows clearly the perimeter frame, which is raised above the wheels, and the slight offset of the engine, to maximise space around the entrance area. The exhaust pipe and fuel tank have yet to be fitted. Ailsa

The first completed Ailsa wore the livery of Alexander Midland. It is seen leaving Glasgow's Killermont Street bus station in March 1974 in its first week in service, operating from Midland's Milngavie depot. Note the bright moulding at skirt level, a characteristic of most Alexander AV bodies.
Stewart J. Brown

The bus later displayed both Volvo and Ailsa badges. The panel to the right of the Ailsa name could be illuminated to show when the bus was being operated without a conductor, so that boarding passengers would be ready to pay the driver at a time when most double-deckers were still crew-operated. This is a June 1974 view at an Omnibus Society event in Glasgow, with the unique Leyland National Suburban Express in the background.
Stewart J. Brown

engine at the rear meant that there was room for an extra row of seats in the lower saloon.

The AV-style body had peaked domes front and rear, and this would become the standard style of Alexander body on the Ailsa — with just 15 exceptions — until the introduction of the RV type in 1981. All Alexander-bodied Ailsas — and most others too — featured the chassis manufacturer's standard radiator grille, which was the same as that used on the Volvo F88 truck. This was hinged at the top to give lift-up access to the radiator and the dipstick — although not to the radiator filler, which was located on the offside, just behind the cab door. A cab door was, of course, necessary because of the engine position. The cab was not particularly spacious.

The project was summed up in Ailsa's brochure. 'The Ailsa bus goes back to the basic design which has proved so successful over the years, with the engine in the tried and proven place — at the front. … The Ailsa double-deck bus is designed to bring back the "good old days" of reliable public transport which can operate at economic levels.'

For the Scottish Bus Group there was just one small problem — the AV body was a full 14ft 6in (4.8m) high, compared with a nominal 13ft 6in (4.5m) for virtually all of the Group's 1,200 double-deckers in the early 1970s. The problem was not simply one of route restrictions; low-height buses were in fact only required on a small number of double-deck routes. A complicating factor was that many of SBG's depots could not accommodate highbridge buses, and this would restrict the allocation of Ailsas.

Before launching its new model Ailsa spoke to Scotland's other major operators — the municipal fleets at Aberdeen, Dundee, Edinburgh and Glasgow. Glasgow, which was having problems with the reliability of its Atlanteans, expressed an interest and indicated it would buy 10 for evaluation. Chief Engineer Alan Westwell was of the view that it was necessary to run a reasonable-sized batch of trial buses. His experience elsewhere had shown that if there were just one or two experimental buses in a fleet they tended not to be a high priority for attention if anything went wrong. However, in June 1973 Glasgow Corporation was absorbed by Greater Glasgow PTE, and the arrival as Director General of Ronald Cox, previously General Manager of Edinburgh Corporation, put paid to the planned 10-bus trial.

After being exhibited at the 1973 Scottish Motor Show the first Ailsa was registered THS 273M (a Renfrewshire mark which reflected the Barrhead base of Ailsa Trucks) and entered service with Midland in March 1974, running from the company's Milngavie depot, on the north-west edge of Glasgow. This was conveniently close — about 10 miles — to the

Ailsa Trucks depot should the as yet unproven design turn out to be troublesome.

The demonstrator was tried by a number of operators in the UK, and by CIE in Dublin. In 1979 it would be rebuilt with full-depth sliding windows and flat-glass windscreens for shipment first to Bangkok, as a demonstrator, and thence to Hong Kong, where it was the first vehicle for a new operator, Citybus.

The compact Volvo engine did not intrude noticeably into the entrance area, and passenger circulation was assisted by having the three-leaf door open forwards, clear of the gangway. This is the original prototype. Note the absence of a bulkhead behind the door. Ailsa

The absence of an engine at the rear made the back end of the Ailsa much neater than any of its contemporaries. The flap on the rear beside the nearside light cluster gave access to the battery isolator switch. Ailsa

Production begins

2 CHAPTER

Ailsa production started with a batch of 10 chassis built in 1974, all bodied by Alexander. These went to four of the seven Passenger Transport Executives, three each going to Greater Glasgow (instead of 10 as originally envisaged), Tyne & Wear and West Midlands, and one to West Yorkshire.

The first to enter service, at the end of 1974, were the three for West Midlands PTE, which were operated initially from Perry Bar depot in Birmingham. One was in the demonstration park at that year's Commercial Motor Show, at London's Earl's Court. Most of WMPTE's buses at this time were Daimler Fleetlines.

Inside Earl's Court there was the first of the three Greater Glasgow buses. These differed from the other Ailsas in the initial batch in that they had panoramic side windows — a requirement of PTE Director General Ronald Cox, who had introduced this feature on Atlanteans in Edinburgh and then brought the idea with him to Glasgow. The Ailsas entered service from Larkfield garage in the spring of 1975. The PTE had adopted the purchasing

policy of its predecessor, Glasgow Corporation, continuing to buy Alexander-bodied Atlanteans. Glasgow had been an early convert to the Atlantean, taking large numbers from 1962, and when the three Ailsas entered service there were around 1,000 Atlanteans — and little else — in the PTE fleet.

The three Tyne & Wear PTE buses entered service in June 1975. Initially based at Byker depot in Newcastle, they were later moved to Sunderland. They differed from other Ailsas in having hydraulic rather than air brakes. Tyne & Wear was no stranger to Alexander bodywork, which was fitted to many of its Atlanteans. Like Glasgow, Newcastle Corporation — the PTE's largest constituent — had switched to Atlanteans at an early date, and the three Ailsas were the first front-engined buses for the fleet since a batch of Leyland PD3s in 1957, the best part of 20 years earlier. Also purchased for evaluation at the same time as the Ailsas were the first of 140 Scania/MCW Metropolitans, the PTE deciding that these were a better bet — although history proved otherwise, as the

The first operator-owned Ailsas to enter service did so with West Midlands PTE at the end of 1974. These had Alexander AV bodies with opening front windows on the upper deck. The open door shows the two-step entrance, an acceptable layout on an urban bus in the 1970s. At this time West Midlands used fareboxes, one of which is visible through the nearside windscreen. Non-standard features of the WMPTE bodies included the use of separate sidelights and indicator units, the latter located on the corner of the body above the windscreen, and a large number of opening windows.
The PTE's 50 production Ailsas exhibited noticeable differences on the front of the body. Stewart J. Brown

10

Left and below: **The first three Ailsas for Greater Glasgow entered service in the spring of 1975. The first was exhibited at the 1974 Commercial Motor Show and carried Volvo lettering on the grille, to which an Ailsa badge had been added by the time it entered service. Only Greater Glasgow took Alexander AV bodies with panoramic windows, which were a feature of its Atlantean deliveries between 1974 and 1980. Because of the front-mounted engine it was necessary to provide a separate cab door for the driver — which was a bit of a squeeze for those of a larger build. Glasgow classified its Ailsas 'AV' ('Ailsa Volvo'), 'A' being used for AEC Regents.**
T. W. Moore, Stewart J. Brown

The Tyne & Wear Ailsas differed from all other Ailsas in having hydraulic rather than air brakes and had short lives with the PTE, operating from the summer of 1975 until 1978. This is a 1978 view in Sunderland, following a repaint from the mainly cream livery in which the buses were delivered. All three were sold to Independent Coachways, of Leeds. Stewart J. Brown

The last of the 10 pre-production Ailsas to enter service did so with the West Yorkshire PTE in August 1975. It was based at Halifax and displayed the PTE's Metro Calderdale local fleetname. Although outwardly similar to the other 10 buses it was unique in having a rearward-ascending staircase. It remained a non-standard bus in the PTE fleet and was sold to Derby City Transport after just six years. Stewart J. Brown

Metropolitans had short lives thanks to serious corrosion problems. The three Tyne & Wear Ailsas were withdrawn after just three years, the shortest-lived with their original operator of any of the pre-production buses.

The solitary West Yorkshire Ailsa was the last to enter service and was based at Halifax. It had been expected to be ready to enter service in the middle of 1975 but did not do so until August. The N-suffix registration originally allocated to it was surrendered, and it took to the streets with a P registration. It differed from other Alexander-bodied Ailsas in that it had a rearward-ascending staircase and seats on the offside front of the top deck, above the driver. It was delivered at a time when most of the West Yorkshire PTE's buses were Atlanteans and Fleetlines with Roe bodies. The Ailsa had a relatively short life with the PTE, being sold to Derby City Transport in 1981.

Not surprisingly in the light of its involvement in the model's development, the Scottish Bus Group was first to place a sizeable order for the Ailsa — for 40 vehicles for Alexander Fife, announced in 1974. In its annual report for that year SBG noted: 'Operational experience with a prototype … has justified the Group in placing considerable orders.' The Fife Ailsas were delivered in 1975, the first being exhibited by Volvo at that year's UITP Congress in Nice. Allocated initially to Aberhill, Dunfermline and Kirkcaldy, they represented the biggest single delivery of double-deckers in the company's

history. Indeed, in 1975 Fife operated just 150 double-deckers, so the Ailsas replaced a quarter of its double-deck fleet. Ultimately Ailsas would be found at most Fife depots.

Greater Glasgow PTE quickly ordered a further 15 Ailsas, which joined the three 1974 buses at the PTE's Larkfield garage at the end of 1975. These not only had panoramic windows but also had conventional rounded domes front and rear, a style which matched the bodies on the PTE's Atlanteans. Glasgow's initial 18 Ailsas were the only examples to feature panoramic-windowed Alexander bodies, and the 15 delivered in 1975 had the only AV bodies with rounded rather than peaked domes. GGPTE was a major Atlantean buyer and in trying the Ailsas — and a batch of 40 Metropolitans, also delivered in 1975 — was perhaps warning Leyland not to take its business for granted. In any event it continued to standardise on the Atlantean, at least until a change in top management in 1979.

In the 1970s the National Bus Company had two standard double-deck models — the Bristol VRT and the Leyland Atlantean AN68. The VRT had either a Gardner 6LXB or Leyland 501 engine; the Atlantean used the Leyland 680, as indicated by the '68' in its chassis designation. However, NBC was prepared to evaluate alternatives and at the end of 1975 took five Ailsas, which were delivered to Maidstone & District, where they ran alongside an identical

The first big delivery of Ailsas saw 40 entering service with Alexander Fife between July and September 1975, marking the biggest influx of new double-deckers in the company's history. A further 50 were ordered for 1977, but of these only six were delivered to Fife, the remainder being allocated to other companies in the Scottish Bus Group.
Stewart J. Brown

number of Scania/MCW Metropolitans — initially in Hastings, later in the Medway Towns. NBC would order no more of either type. The Ailsas were sold in 1982, and all would at some time see service with A1 Service in Scotland.

Towards the end of 1975 the first Ailsa was exported, a solitary Alexander-bodied bus for China Motor Bus in Hong Kong. This was the first Alexander body for Hong Kong; the first of many, as it would transpire. As in Scotland, operators in Hong Kong had reservations about the reliability of rear-engined double-deckers, although their choice for a new generation of front-engined models would focus on vehicles with the trusty 10.45-litre Gardner 6LXB engine — the Leyland (Guy) Victory and Dennis Jubilant — rather than the 6.7-litre-engined Ailsa. Exports would play an important part in the Ailsa story — but not to Hong Kong.

The first CMB Ailsa was a 79-seater. It featured a Scottish-style triangular destination display and had opening flat-glass windscreens in place of the fixed curved glass which was standard on the Alexander AV body. A second bus for CMB followed in 1976, and in 1978 came a batch of six 107-seaters — the highest seating capacity of any Ailsas, achieved by extending the rear overhang, increasing the vehicles' length to 34ft (10.3m), and the use of 3+2 seating, the split being 62/45. One was exhibited at the 1978 Motor Show. These were the days before Hong

Kong's buses featured air-conditioning, and the AV-style bodies for CMB had full-depth sliding windows. The first two Ailsas were delivered in CMB's red and cream livery; the later vehicles were in the new blue and cream colour scheme. While the first CMB Ailsa had an essentially standard AV body with a normal full-width entrance, the other seven were built to CMB's preferred layout, with a narrow entrance and a full-width exit immediately aft of the front axle. These buses had 201bhp engines and SCG gearboxes, apart from the last vehicle, which had a Voith gearbox, by that time available as an option. Most of CMB's eight two-axle Ailsas would be withdrawn in 1989, but the longest-lived survived until 1991.

While the initial SBG order for 40 buses was important, it was hardly a surprise. A more significant 1975 order came from West Midlands PTE. Here the standard bus was the Daimler Fleetline, but the combination of huge orders from London Transport and disruption caused by the transfer of chassis production from Coventry to Leyland meant that there were long delays in delivering Fleetlines. Against this background the PTE placed the biggest order yet for the new Ailsa: 50 with Alexander bodies. These were delivered in the first six months of 1976. Whereas most operators accepted Alexander's standard curved windscreens, the buses for West Midlands had flat-glass screens, to reduce replacement costs. The upper-deck front windows were different too, with opening top sections. The buses were allocated initially to two former Midland Red garages, Oldbury and Sutton Coldfield, but ultimately all would be based at Perry Barr, in Birmingham.

Another big order soon followed, again motivated in part by the problems Leyland was having in supplying chassis. This came from South Yorkshire PTE, which ordered no fewer than 62 Ailsas. The intention had been that these should have Alexander bodywork, but the Scottish builder couldn't deliver finished vehicles quickly enough. Instead the PTE turned to a new bodybuilder, Van Hool McArdle, based in the Republic of Ireland, which built a stylish dual-door 75-seat design. The initial order was for 42 bodies, but this was soon increased to 62. These were the first Ailsas to be bodied by a builder other than Alexander. They were ordered as 76-seaters, but when the first vehicle failed its tilt test one seat was removed from the front upper deck. Most were delivered in 1976, the final few arriving in the early months of 1977. Van Hool exhibited an SYPTE Ailsa at the Brussels Commercial Vehicle Show in January 1977. One bus, which was badly damaged on delivery, had to be returned to the factory and did not enter service until January 1978 after

A further 15 Ailsas were delivered to the Greater Glasgow PTE towards the end of 1975. They had panoramic windows, like the first three, but also had conventional rounded domes, front and rear, as specified on the PTE's Alexander-bodied Atlanteans. These were the only AV bodies of this style.
Stewart J. Brown

The National Bus Company was committed to buying products from Leyland-group companies in which it had a financial interest, but it still evaluated other makes and models, including five Ailsas. These joined the Maidstone & District fleet in December 1975 and were operated first in Hastings and later in the Medway Towns, where this one is seen in May 1982. All five would be sold later that year. Stewart J. Brown

being shown in the demonstration park at the Scottish Motor Show in November 1977. This bus had a Voith automatic gearbox, while the rest of the batch were supplied with the standard SCG unit. One vehicle operated for a short time with a Fiat/SRN gearbox. SYPTE opted for the higher-powered (201bhp) version of the TD70 engine to cope with Sheffield's hilly terrain.

The first SYPTE bus was actually bodied by Van Hool in Belgium; the production bodies were assembled in the former CIE works in Dublin, which had been taken over by Van Hool McArdle. The bodies on the Ailsa were of a striking design with deep curved windscreens on both decks and much larger side windows than on the Alexander AV body. Unlike the Alexander body, which used aluminium framing, the Van Hool McArdle body was steel-framed, which led to corrosion appearing late in the vehicles' lives.

The Van Hool McArdle Ailsas were arguably the most attractive double-deckers of the 1970s. Indeed, it would not be until 1991 and the launch of the Optare Spectra that another double-decker quite as stylish would appear in Britain.

Another significant order for the Ailsa came from Tayside Regional Transport (now headed by Alan Westwell, who had moved from Glasgow), which took 35 in 1976. An initial batch of five was delivered in April, to be followed by 30 which entered service from August onwards. These had Alexander bodies but of dual-door layout, which reduced the seating capacity to 75. Tayside had taken over the Dundee municipal fleet in 1975, and the Ailsas were the first buses to be delivered in Tayside's new livery of two-tone blue and white. Subsequently Tayside took delivery of 25 Alexander-bodied Bristol VRTs, which arrived in the early months of 1977. But, in what had an uncanny echo of SBG's experience with the VRT at the start of the 1970s, most of Tayside's Bristols would be short-lived, more than half being sold by 1982. The Ailsas, on the other hand, were a success, repeat orders soon being placed, and Tayside would ultimately operate the UK's largest fleet of the type.

One of Tayside's 1976 Ailsas was used for a few months as a demonstrator and was also tested by *Commercial Motor* magazine. It received a generally positive review, tester Martin Watkins noting that 'the handling and

CMB's first Ailsa had a modified version of the standard Alexander AV body with a conventional full-width entrance and an SBG-style destination display. It had full-depth sliding windows and flat-glass windscreens with an opening section for ventilation. It is seen (right) being loaded at Southampton docks in late 1975 and (below) in rather better weather on the streets of Hong Kong.
Brian Simpson,
Ian Allan Library

steering were among the best I have come across'. He also praised the ride, but was critical of the gearchange quality on the SCG gearbox with CAV fully automatic control. In comparing the Ailsa with a Leyland-engined Bristol VRT which he had tested, Watkins noted that 'the Ailsa, even with its smaller engine, flew up all the hills that had reduced the Bristol to near crawling pace', this on a cross-country run between Leicester and Oxford. But he wasn't too impressed with the brakes, at least on simulated urban operation, where he noted that he could smell them overheating and also experienced some brake fade. Fully laden, the Ailsa returned just under 5mpg on local running in Leicester but just over 10mpg on the run to Oxford using the M1 and A43 roads — leading to the test report's title, 'An economical bus on the long run'. The overall average for the 107-mile test was 7.5mpg. *Commercial Motor* quoted list prices for the Ailsa of £14,353 for the chassis and £12,750 for the Alexander body, a total of £27,103. The same vehicle was also tested by *Buses* magazine, which recorded fuel figures of 9.8mpg on inter-urban running and 6.75mpg when making four stops per mile.

With big orders from South Yorkshire, West Midlands and Tayside, 1976 was the best year for Ailsa deliveries in the UK, 145 entering service. This compares with an average of 65 a year over the model's 11-year life on the British market.

The six Ailsas which joined the CMB fleet in 1978 had an extended rear overhang which increased their length from 9.85 to 10.3m. There is an additional short window at the rear of the Alexander body, which seated 107 passengers.
Ian Allan Library

The 50 Ailsas delivered to West Midlands PTE between December 1975 and May 1976 had Alexander bodies with some minor changes to meet the PTE's requirements. Most obvious were the flat-glass windscreens, which were cheaper to replace than the standard curved style. The front upper-deck windows were also different from the standard items, and a raised moulding was provided to accommodate the PTE's standard destination display. T. W. Moore

The first Ailsas to be bodied by a builder other than Alexander were 62 with Van Hool McArdle bodies for South Yorkshire PTE. With their big side windows and deep windscreens, these were striking vehicles. In this pre-delivery view the first vehicle to be built in Ireland has been temporarily fitted with Dublin destination blinds and shows its fleet number in the route-number display.
Ian Allan Library

Van Hool McArdle also managed to incorporate a more generously sized cab door than that used by Alexander. As this photograph shows, the Van Hool McArdle bodies had seats at the front offside of the upper deck, unlike the majority of Alexander-bodied Ailsas. Most of the South Yorkshire vehicles were delivered in 1976 and withdrawn in 1986 as the PTE reduced its fleet in readiness for deregulation.
Stewart J. Brown

Tayside would become the biggest operator of Ailsas in Britain, placing initial orders for 35 which were delivered in 1976. This was the fleet's first Ailsa, one of a batch of five, with dual-door Alexander body.
Gavin Booth collection

The remaining 30 Ailsas delivered to Tayside in 1976 were similar to the first five apart from some minor revisions to the front fibre-glass moulding, which had been altered to incorporate the headlamps and foglamps in a raised section and dispensed with the separate front bumper of earlier bodies. One spent some time as a demonstrator, being seen here in Edinburgh in October 1976 running for Lothian Region Transport. LRT, however, was not swayed by the Ailsa's merits and remained loyal to the Leyland Atlantean.
Stewart J. Brown

Winning new customers

The first Ailsas for an independent operator — A1 Service — entered service in the summer of 1976. These were three Alexander-bodied buses. Three more Alexander-bodied Ailsas would be delivered to A1 in 1978, and again in 1979. One of the first A1 chassis was exhibited at the 1975 Scottish Motor Show. A1 also took the only other Ailsas to be bodied by Van Hool McArdle, two SYPTE-style dual-door buses delivered in 1977 and built along with the last of South Yorkshire's batch.

The only Ailsa for an English independent operator was an Alexander-bodied bus delivered to Premier of Stainforth in 1976, for use on the company's service to Doncaster. There was another one-off for service in England, an Alexander-bodied bus for the Hanley Crouch Community Association in Islington, north London. It was delivered in 1978 in Tayside-style two-tone blue and white. When it was replaced by a new Citybus in 1989 Hanley Crouch's Ailsa found further employment with independent operators in the South West of England.

One chassis built in 1975 was unique. It featured a modified frame to accommodate low-height bodywork, the main side and cross-members being lowered to be level with the central spine instead of located above it. The central spine was therefore built in three sections, between the cross-members. The front axle was also modified to allow the gangway to be lower, and the wheel-arch areas of the perimeter frame were box sections rather than the normal channel section, to provide added strength. Shallower fuel tanks were fitted too, but without any reduction in capacity.

The chassis was designated B55-20 (the standard chassis being a B55-10). It was bodied by Alexander to an overall height of 13ft 8in (4.2m) and delivered to Derby City Transport at the start of 1977. It was the first new Ailsa for an English municipal fleet. The Alexander body looked like a combination of the standard AV upper-deck structure married to the lower deck of Alexander's AD-type low-height body. This meant that the lower-deck windows were

A1 of Ardrossan was one of only two independent operators to buy new Ailsas, taking 11 between 1976 and 1979. Nine of these had Alexander bodywork, among them this 1978 bus seen in Irvine, a mile or so from the Volvo plant where the chassis was built.
Stewart J. Brown

The only Van Hool McArdle double-deck bodies supplied to a British operator other than South Yorkshire PTE were two on Ailsas which were delivered to A1 in March 1977. One passes through Saltcoats, on A1's trunk service between Ardrossan and Kilmarnock, later that year.
Stewart J. Brown

shallower than those on the upper deck, giving the vehicle a strangely top-heavy look. It featured flat-glass windscreens, similar to those on the buses supplied to the West Midlands PTE and to Hong Kong. Seating capacity was 77, two fewer than normal. There was a bulge on the roof to provide the legally required headroom at the top of the stairs and above the first rows of seats, which were slightly higher than the rest.

Derby used the vehicle mainly on the former Blue Bus service to Burton-upon-Trent, which passed under a low bridge at Willington.

The Scottish Bus Group had been planning to order 18 low-height Ailsas — 12 for Alexander Northern and six for Highland — but when it saw the cramped interior layout of the bus being built for Derby decided not to proceed, instead buying extra Ford single-deckers.

Just one English independent — Premier, of Stainforth, near Doncaster — bought a new Ailsa. Fitted with a standard 79-seat Alexander body, the bus entered service in August 1976.
Gavin Booth collection

Not strictly an independent operator, the Islington-based Hanley Crouch Community Association purchased a solitary Alexander-bodied Ailsa in 1978. It is seen here when new with a group of elderly ladies demonstrating 1970s fashions. The livery was the same as that used by Tayside. Ian Allan Library

A part-built bus was exhibited at the 1976 Commercial Motor Show as Ailsa sought to develop export sales. Metal Sections specialised in body kits for local assembly by overseas operators and demonstrated this with a simple type of body — with a Hong Kong-style single-width entrance — on the Ailsa underframe. The project went nowhere, and the part-built body was dismantled. The chassis passed to Tayside in 1977 as part of an Alexander-bodied batch. Gavin Booth collection

At the 1976 Commercial Motor Show, the last to be held at Earl's Court, Metal Sections, the specialist supplier of body kits to overseas operators, showed a part-built body on an Ailsa chassis. The body was never completed, and the chassis — with an Allison rather than SCG gearbox — was supplied to Tayside as the last of a batch of Alexander-bodied buses delivered in 1977.

In the autumn of 1977 a Mk II version of the Ailsa was announced. The most obvious difference was that the driving position was raised — clearly identifiable on Alexander-bodied buses by the higher position of the windscreen. The front brake shoes were increased in width, and the kingpins redesigned to give a longer life. The Hamworthy rear axle was modified to address complaints about noise and reliability, and the SCG gearbox now came with CAV fully-automatic control as standard. Voith and Allison automatic gearboxes were offered as options. There was also additional sound-proofing around the engine.

Two English municipal fleets almost ordered Ailsas in the late 1970s. Cleveland Transit was considering an order for 30 or 40 — but did not proceed with it. To speed delivery of new buses and the expansion of one-man operation Ipswich Borough Transport was planning to dual-source new double-deckers, buying both Ailsas and Atlanteans. However, Leyland convinced Ipswich that it could deliver all of its requirements on time, and squeezed Ailsa out.

Having got the Ailsa project going, SBG was a bit slow in placing orders. The first 40 had entered service with Fife in 1975, but there were no double-deckers at all in the group's 1976 orders. In 1977 it ordered 100 double-deckers, divided equally between Fleetlines for Western SMT and further Ailsas for Fife. Bearing in mind that Fife operated only 150 double-deckers,

Left and below: **A unique low-height Ailsa was supplied to Derby City Transport in February 1977. The combination of deep windows on the upper deck and shallow windows on the lower deck gave it an ungainly appearance, and the first four rows of upper-deck seats were higher than the rest — visible in the nearside photograph — which required a bulge in the roof. The flat-glass windscreen was similar to those specified by West Midlands PTE. It is seen in service in Derby bus station in April 1978 and then two months later at Showbus at Woburn Abbey after a repaint and subtle change of fleetname; Derby had become a city in June 1977.** Stewart J. Brown

Right and below right:
The chassis of the
low-height Ailsa, showing
clearly the perimeter frame,
a feature of all Ailsas,
and the low build of this
unique vehicle in which the
cross-members ran the full
width of the chassis at the
same height as the central
spine, rather than being
located above it. Ailsa

this was a surprising order, and before delivery commenced there was a change of plan, the majority of the Ailsas being reallocated. Fife got just six, the remaining 44 being shared between other SBG fleets. Alexander Midland received 14, while Central SMT, Eastern Scottish and Western SMT got 10 each. The first 20 (for Midland and Fife) were delivered in May 1977, while all but one of the remaining 30 appeared between February and June 1978 as Alexander struggled to cope with a backlog of orders. One of the Western vehicles was completed ahead of the rest and exhibited at the 1977 Scottish Motor Show.

The Midland vehicles, operated initially on city services in Perth, were to be that company's only Ailsas; subsequent double-deck deliveries would comprise Leyland Fleetlines and MCW Metrobuses. The 10 Central vehicles were based at East Kilbride and operated on routes into Glasgow. They were the company's first new double-deckers since the aforementioned batch of Fleetlines, which had been delivered in 1971 — and despatched to other SBG companies four years later. Western's were allocated to the Paisley area, while those for Eastern were based at Musselburgh and Dalkeith, two depots able to accommodate highbridge buses.

There were only 30 double-deckers — none of them Ailsas — in SBG's 1978 orders, but for 1979 the group ordered 40 Ailsas, out of a total double-deck requirement of 94 vehicles. These were SBG's first Mk II models and were shared equally between Central and Fife. Central's 1979 Ailsas were delivered in a non-standard livery with a much larger area of cream relief.

Tayside's 1979 intake of 21 Ailsas included six Mk II models. The last had a Voith gearbox in place of the usual SCG unit and was displayed by Volvo at the UITP Congress in Helsinki. In 1983 one of the Mk IIs would be converted to open-top — the only Ailsa to be so treated.

The Mk II was a short-lived model, being superseded by the Mk III, which was announced at the 1980 Motor Show. This used a new Volvo-designed rear axle, the EV85, with a stronger differential of a design that ruled out building a low-height version of the Ailsa. The frame was modified to reduce the floor level by 40mm, while the gearbox and fuel tank were repositioned to improve weight distribution by further reducing the loading on the front axle. The cross-members on the frame were relocated to facilitate wider pillar spacing — Alexander bodies on the Mk III would be of the new R-type design. There were also modifications to the TD70 engine, intended to improve fuel economy. Air-over-leaf suspension was now available as an option — although the initial installation was troublesome and required some re-working to get it right.

At the start of 1980 SBG ran a trial at Midland in which it compared four models — an Ailsa, an MCW Metrobus, a Leyland Fleetline and a Dennis Dominator. The buses were operated from Milngavie depot — where the original Ailsa had been based back in 1974 — and the Ailsa came bottom of the list on fuel economy, achieving 5.57mpg, the three Gardner-engined buses returning 5.86mpg (Dennis), 6.26mpg (MCW) and 7.08mpg (Leyland). These figures compare badly with an earlier trial by Western in Greenock, where the original Ailsa demonstrator had achieved 7.5mpg, compared with 8.0mpg for a Fleetline.

Whatever enthusiasm there had been within SBG for the Ailsa back in 1973 was clearly waning, in part because of changes in the group's top management and in particular the retirement in 1977 of Engineering Director Roddy Mackenzie. In five years the group had taken just 130 Ailsas, and orders slowed further in the 1980s. In 1980 there were 24 Mk IIs for Western, which were the last British Ailsas to have Alexander AV bodies. They were followed in 1981 by 20 of the upgraded Mk III for Eastern, with Alexander's new RV body. The RV could seat up to 81 passengers, accommodating two more in the lower saloon. One of the Eastern buses was exhibited at the 1981 Scottish Motor Show.

Fortunately, as SBG's interest was waning, a new customer appeared. In 1979 Greater Glasgow PTE — which became Strathclyde PTE in 1980 — had appointed a new Director General, Tayside's Alan Westwell. He brought with him his pro-Ailsa vehicle policy, placing orders for a total of 40 Ailsas with Alexander RV-type bodies for delivery in 1981. The first was exhibited at the UITP Congress in Dublin in May, while the last was shown at the Scottish Motor Show in Glasgow in November. Follow-on orders were soon placed for a further 41, which were delivered in 1982, and then 35, delivered in 1983. Of the 1982 buses 20 had SCG gearboxes, and 21 Voith; all subsequent Ailsas for Strathclyde had Voith transmission. A final batch of 15 was delivered in 1984, giving Strathclyde a fleet of 131 broadly similar Alexander-bodied Ailsas. The 1983/4 batches were delivered in the PTE's new orange and black livery, the earlier batches having arrived in the short-lived yellow, green and black scheme. The 1984 buses were the last Ailsas to be delivered in the UK, entering service in

November of that year. Ailsas would serve Glasgow — latterly with First, as successor to the PTE's bus operation — until 2006.

With busy routes running 24 hours a day, operators in Hong Kong were looking at bigger buses at the start of the 1980s, which saw their British suppliers — Dennis, Leyland and MCW — developing three-axle versions of their existing chassis. Although Ailsa had supplied just eight vehicles to CMB, it decided to pursue this potential new market and built two three-axle chassis for CMB. These had 12m-long Alexander RV bodies with 101 seats (split 74/27) and a total capacity of 170 passengers. The third axle — a steering axle, behind the drive axle — permitted not only an increase in length but also a higher gross vehicle weight. The buses were delivered in 1981 and would remain in service until 1998. Also in 1981 an Alexander-bodied Ailsa was shipped to Singapore for demonstration to Singapore Bus Services, but this elicited no orders.

In the mid-1970s Ailsas had been delivered to five of the seven PTEs — Greater Glasgow, Tyne & Wear, South Yorkshire, West Midlands and West Yorkshire. The remaining two, Greater Manchester and Merseyside, purchased Ailsas for evaluation in the 1980s.

In August 1980 Greater Manchester took delivery of a solitary Ailsa Mk II with bodywork by Northern Counties, the PTE's preferred supplier. The chassis had been built in 1978, and it took Northern Counties the best part of two years to get around to adapting its body to fit the Ailsa. The bus, a 79-seater, appeared in the demonstration park at the 1980 Motor Show and entered service as a crew-operated vehicle in Stockport in January 1981. Orders were placed by the PTE for four more Ailsas, by now Mk III models. Two, also bodied by Northern Counties, were added to the fleet in 1982 and allocated to Wigan, where they were soon joined by the original vehicle. This latter was delivered in GMPTE's SELNEC-inspired orange and white livery, whereas the two later vehicles arrived in the brown, orange and white livery which had been adopted at the end of 1980. The last two Ailsas were cancelled by the PTE. GM Buses, the PTE's post-1986 operating company, kept the three Ailsas until 1990.

In 1982 Volvo had four stock Ailsa chassis bodied by Marshall. Two — the chassis cancelled by Greater Manchester — were sold to Derby City Transport, although before being delivered they spent a short time running for Merseyside PTE, painted in PTE livery. The other two remained unsold until the spring of 1984, when they were purchased by Strathclyde PTE. One further Ailsa was bodied by Marshall — as a unique 11m-long 51-seat single-decker. It too

The Scottish Bus Group ordered 50 Ailsas for delivery in 1977. Originally all were to go to Alexander Fife, but this plan was quickly changed. The first 14 were delivered to Alexander Midland in May 1977, as were six for Fife. Destined to be Midland's only Ailsas, they were used initially on city services in Perth, where one is seen during its first week in operation. Stewart J. Brown

The remaining 30 of SBG's 1977 Ailsas were not delivered until 1978 and were shared equally between Central SMT, Eastern Scottish and Western SMT, being the first of their type for all three companies. An Eastern bus enters Edinburgh's Princes Street in the summer of 1978. Stewart J. Brown

A Central bus, in original livery but with SBG's corporate fleetname, adopted during 1978, arrives at Glasgow's Buchanan Bus Station in 1985. Stewart J. Brown

Western's Ailsas operated in the Paisley area and wore an attractive new version of the company's livery, with cream window surrounds on the lower deck. Stewart J. Brown

The last examples of what might be called the Mk I Ailsa were 15 with Alexander AV bodies for Tayside, delivered in 1979. They took the number of Ailsas operated by Tayside to 70, out of a total fleet of 240 buses. This one is seen when new. Stewart J. Brown

joined the Strathclyde fleet, in the early months of 1983. However, whilst this was the only *purpose-built* single-decker it was not the only single-deck Ailsa, for in 1985 one of Strathclyde's 1975 double-deckers was rebuilt thus after losing an argument with a low bridge.

The two Marshall-bodied buses for Derby were followed by 13 with bodywork by Northern Counties. These entered service in 1982, joining the solitary low-height bus of 1977 and the former West Yorkshire vehicle, which had been acquired in 1981.

In 1980 West Midlands PTE intended to order a further 50 Alexander-bodied Ailsas to compensate for Leyland's inability to supply Titans which were on order, but this plan was

The Alexander-bodied Mk II Ailsa was easily recognisable by its raised windscreen, necessary to match the raised driving position. Central SMT received 20 Mk IIs in 1979, the only buses delivered with this style of livery incorporating cream on the area between decks. This is a 1980 view. The bus is crew-operated; the conductor is standing by the door. Stewart J. Brown

over-ruled by West Midlands County Council, which sought to protect local employment by having the PTE buy buses from MCW. Despite this, in the summer of 1981 WMPTE evaluated a Mk III Ailsa destined for Strathclyde PTE, which was painted in full WMPTE livery and delivered direct to West Midlands. It was also tried by Merseyside PTE, still in West Midlands livery, before being delivered to Strathclyde in December. Merseyside then took delivery of two Mk IIIs with Alexander RV bodies in 1982, and these were followed by 13 similar vehicles in 1984. Twelve of Merseyside's 15 Ailsas would be sold to Cardiff Bus in 1996.

Tayside continued to buy Ailsas in the 1980s, but not all with Alexander bodies. In 1980 it took its last Ailsas with the original AV-style Alexander body, these being a batch of 35 Mk IIs. The first 20 had dual-door bodywork, as on previous deliveries, the remainder single-door. They were followed in 1981 by 15 RV-bodied Mk IIIs, after which Tayside switched its body orders to Northern Counties, which supplied 10 dual-door buses in the spring of 1983, and to East Lancs, which delivered 25, also of dual-door layout, in the same year. All of Tayside's Mk IIIs — including the Alexander-bodied buses — were 10.3m long, rather than the standard 9.85m, the extra length being in the rear overhang. This allowed for an extra row of seats in the upper saloon and for the provision of a separate exit door without any loss of lower-deck seating capacity compared with a standard-length bus. Those with East Lancs bodywork

were the only Ailsas to be bodied by the Blackburn-based builder. Northern Counties normally fitted its own style of front grille on Ailsas, but the bodies it built for Tayside used the standard Ailsa grille. All of Tayside's Mk IIIs had Voith gearboxes. Tayside's last Ailsas were withdrawn from regular service in 1999, by which time the company was owned by National Express, and most of the dual-door buses had had their centre exits removed.

The first — and only — buyer of new Ailsas in Wales was Cardiff City Transport. After evaluating a Tayside bus Cardiff ordered a total of 36, and these were delivered in three batches — 18 in the spring of 1982, nine at the end of that year, and the final nine in the winter of 1983/4. All were bodied by Northern Counties, making Cardiff the biggest user of the Ailsa/Northern Counties combination. After problems with its previous big bus order — for Bristol VRTs — Cardiff decided not to put all its eggs in one basket and split its new bus order, so alongside the 36 Ailsas it took 36 Leyland Olympians.

After a gap of three years SBG took delivery of its last Ailsas in 1984. It ordered 20 — 10 each for Fife and Eastern. In the end Fife received only eight, the last two being cancelled in favour of Citybuses. Those for Eastern were among the few B-registered Ailsas; the only others were the final 15 delivered to Strathclyde.

Perhaps the biggest surprise as the Ailsa neared the end of its production life came with the delivery in 1984 of three examples to

There were 20 Mk IIs for Alexander Fife in 1979, and these would be the company's last Ailsas until 1984, when it received eight Mk IIIs. Stewart J. Brown

In 1980 the Scottish Bus Group carried out comparative trials at the Milngavie depot of Alexander Midland. These used four vehicles — from the left a 1978 Fleetline, a 1979 Metrobus, a 1979 Mk II Ailsa and a 1978 Dennis Dominator. The Ailsa came from the Fife fleet but was repainted in Midland livery for the trial. Gavin Booth collection

The last Mk II Ailsas and the last Alexander AV bodies for the UK were 24 delivered to Western in 1980 For these the livery was again revised, with cream window surrounds on both decks. Like the first 10 Ailsas for Western they operated in the Paisley area. One is seen approaching Paisley Cross in February 1981. Stewart J. Brown

London Buses. This was part of an evaluation of different types of vehicle, which saw the Ailsas running alongside three Leyland Olympians, three Dennis Dominators and two MCW Metrobus Mk IIs. The first two Ailsas entered service from Stockwell depot in April 1984. They had dual-door Alexander bodywork with 78 seats and a sliding cab door, as first seen on buses for Strathclyde PTE. On weekdays they operated on route 170, between Aldwych and Roehampton; on Sundays they were allocated to the 44, which ran from Aldgate to Tooting. They were the first Alexander-bodied buses built for London.

The third London Ailsa was delivered in June 1984 but did not enter service until March 1985 (making it the last Ailsa actually to take to the streets in Britain) and was built to a unique specification with its exit door behind the rear axle — a layout made possible only by the Ailsa's front-mounted engine. This bus had two staircases and just 64 seats, and following opposition from drivers to its use without a conductor it was employed on crew-operated routes, initially the 77A (King's Cross–Wimbledon) and later the 88 (Acton Green–Mitcham). The rear door was soon removed — in the summer of 1986 — resulting in an increase in seating capacity to 68, but the bus retained its two staircases.

All three London Ailsas were transferred to Potters Bar at the end of 1986. The twin-staircase bus was withdrawn in 1992 following an accident, but the other two remained in service

in London until 1995, having passed to MTL London Northern in 1994 when London Buses was privatised.

The real success story for the Ailsa in the 1980s lay not in the UK, where sales were averaging 70 a year, nor in Hong Kong, a traditional market for UK double-deckers where despite Volvo's best efforts the Ailsa was making no impression at all. It was instead in a new market. Between 1981 and 1985 Volvo delivered an impressive 320 Mk III Ailsas to Indonesia, most for operation in Jakarta. Although the Alexander RV-type body had replaced the AV in the UK, the Indonesian Ailsas used the older AV-style body, built to Hong Kong specification with two doors and a lengthened rear overhang. Both chassis and bodies were shipped as kits and assembled in Indonesia.

When production ended in 1985 a total of 716 Ailsas had been built for service in the UK, plus a further 331 for export. The model's principal successes in England — at West Midlands and South Yorkshire PTEs — were in part due to the Leyland organisation's inability to supply chassis quickly enough. The Scottish Bus Group, which had been instrumental in the Ailsa's development, didn't follow through with the volume of orders Ailsa might have anticipated, as, despite its dissatisfaction with the Daimler/Leyland Fleetline, it continued to purchase the model.

Between 1975 and 1984 SBG bought 192 Ailsas — but more than 450 double-deckers of other types, including 204 of the supposedly

The first Mk III Ailsas for the Scottish Bus Group were 20 for Eastern Scottish in 1981, with the new Alexander RV-type body. The frame of the Mk III chassis was revised to suit the wider pillar spacing of the new style of body. Eastern's Ailsas operated in the Edinburgh area.
Stewart J. Brown

After taking 40 Mk III Ailsas in 1981 Strathclyde received a further 41 generally similar buses in 1982. The RV body retained the unusual three-leaf door of the previous AV type. All of Strathclyde's Alexander RV bodies were 79-seaters. Stewart J. Brown

The last Ailsas delivered to a British operator were 15 for Strathclyde in November 1984, which brought to 131 the number of Alexander-bodied Ailsas in the fleet. The later deliveries were in orange and black, a livery which was applied to earlier vehicles when they became due for repaint. When new they had 'Strathclyde Transport' fleetnames; this was changed in 1986 to 'Strathclyde's Buses' when the PTE set up its new operating company in readiness for local bus deregulation. The only other B-registered Ailsas were operated by Eastern Scottish. Stewart J. Brown

unpopular Fleetline. Fife, the biggest SBG Ailsa user, with 74, bought no more Fleetlines after taking Ailsas but did add Leyland Olympians to its fleet in 1983. Central received 30 Ailsas before switching its allegiance to the Dennis Dominator. Eastern also took 30 Ailsas (and would later receive second-hand examples) but also bought 50 Olympians. Western continued buying Fleetlines at the same time as Ailsas (and in larger numbers) and then, like Central, switched to the Dominator.

So there was something of a lukewarm acceptance by SBG companies of the new bus which had been designed for them — in which it is possible to detect echoes of a previous attempt by a manufacturer to build a bus to meet the Group's requirements: the Albion Lowlander. Leyland had wanted SBG to buy low-height Atlanteans at the start of the 1960s, but the Group said no, and as a result the Albion Lowlander was developed. SBG ordered 193 — one more than the number of Ailsas it bought. But at least the Ailsa enjoyed sales successes elsewhere, including one major overseas customer, unlike the Lowlander, which found few customers outside SBG.

The only purpose-built Ailsa single-decker was a Marshall-bodied 51-seater built for stock by Volvo and bought by Strathclyde in 1983. It couldn't compete with more sophisticated rear-engined single-deck models. Stewart J. Brown

Strathclyde also bought two stock Ailsas with 79-seat Marshall double-deck bodies. The chassis had been built in 1981, but the buses did not enter service with Strathclyde until February 1984.
Stewart J. Brown

Above and below: Alongside its new single-deck Ailsa Strathclyde operated a second single-decker, cut down from one of the panoramic-windowed 1975 double-deckers after it struck a low bridge. As part of the rebuild it received an RV-style front end with single-piece windscreen. With the deep cantrail panels it still looked pretty much what it was — a cut-down double-decker. It initially wore the PTE's coach livery but was later repainted in more appropriate bus livery. Gavin Booth, Donald MacRae

A pair of three-axle Ailsas was built for China Motor Bus of Hong Kong in 1981. These had a rear steering axle and 12m-long 101-seat Alexander RV bodies. Although they didn't win any orders they did survive in service for 18 years. One is seen on test with a temporary windscreen fitted, near Alexander's Falkirk factory. Gavin Booth

Greater Manchester PTE took delivery of a solitary Mk II Ailsa in 1980, and had it bodied by its preferred bodybuilder, Northern Counties of Wigan. It was a 79-seater, with four more seats than in Atlanteans being delivered at the same time, and was in the demonstration park at the 1980 Motor Show. It had a cut-down version of the standard Ailsa grille. Stewart J. Brown

Above: In 1981 a Strathclyde PTE Ailsa was painted in West Midlands livery and operated on trial from Oldbury garage from May to August. It then moved on to Merseyside, where it ran for the PTE for a few months, still in West Midlands colours. It is seen here in Liverpool in October 1981. Stewart J. Brown

Left: Merseyside also trialled two Marshall-bodied Ailsas, which were painted in PTE colours but in fact belonged to Derby City Transport. The chassis were from a cancelled Greater Manchester PTE order. Stewart J. Brown

Below: Merseyside did buy 15 Ailsa Mk IIIs for evaluation. All had Alexander bodies. The 13 delivered in 1984 were 81-seaters; the first two, in 1982, seated 78. They operated primarily on the Wirral peninsula, this example being seen in Birkenhead in 1985. Stewart J. Brown

Ahead of the delivery of 15 new Ailsas in 1982 Derby City Transport acquired the solitary example owned by West Yorkshire, in 1981. The high-set destination display had been positioned to accommodate West Yorkshire's livery, which included a band of green relief above the windscreen.
Stewart J. Brown

In 1982 Derby took 13 Mk III Ailsas with Northern Counties bodies featuring the bodybuilder's own radiator grille. This one is seen in the city centre soon after delivery.
Stewart J. Brown

After buying 111 Ailsas with Alexander's original AV-style body Tayside bought only one batch of 15 with the newer RV style. These were delivered in 1981 and looked good in Tayside's livery. Donald MacRae

To mark 800 years of Dundee's existence in 1991, a Tayside Ailsa was repainted in Dundee Corporation livery. The application of the colours, with orange lining, represented a style used in the 1950s. The fleetname between decks was a feature of the city's buses in the 1930s. Donald MacRae

The Northern Counties-bodied Ailsas for Tayside were generally similar to those supplied to Greater Manchester, Derby and Cardiff but had the standard Ailsa grille in place of the smaller version used by Northern Counties for its other customers. The Tayside buses were also longer, at 10.3m. When new this bus had a separate exit door and was finished in Tayside's original livery of two-tone blue and white; this brighter scheme was adopted in 1986 after the operation had been reformed as the council-owned Tayside Public Transport Co.
Donald MacRae

The only Ailsas with East Lancs bodywork were 25 for Tayside in 1983.
Gavin Booth

Cardiff City Transport was a late convert to the Ailsa, taking 36 between 1982 and 1984. Fitted with 74-seat Northern Counties bodywork, they were the only Ailsas new to a Welsh operator. The last examples remained in regular use until December 2007, having served the city for an impressive 25 years.
Stewart J. Brown

Three Alexander-bodied Ailsas joined the London Buses fleet in 1984, for use in comparative trials with buses from Dennis, Leyland and MCW.
Two were conventional dual-door buses, with the exit behind the front axle.
Stewart J. Brown

The third London Ailsa had two staircases and the exit door in the rear overhang, a layout which reduced its seating capacity from 76 to 64. It was not a success, and the rear door was later panelled over. Although delivered in the summer of 1984 it did not enter service until March 1985, becoming the last Ailsa to do so in the UK. *Alexander*

Interior view of the third of London's Ailsas, showing the longitudinal seats over the rear wheels, with a nearside bulkhead and the staircase on the offside. The centrally located rear emergency exit is also visible. Note the flat gangway, and the fact that despite the vehicle's unusual layout there are 20 forward-facing seats, all on the same level — something which would be lost with the adoption of low-floor designs from the late 1990s. A notice beside the front staircase reads: 'To avoid congestion please do not stand near the stairs.' *Alexander*

There was just one big overseas market for the Ailsa. Between 1981 and 1985 a total of 320 — almost a third of all Ailsas sold — were exported to Indonesia. They had Alexander AV-type bodywork built to a similar layout as used on most of those for Hong Kong, with a narrow entrance and a standard-width exit. Both the chassis and the bodies were shipped as kits for local assembly. This view in Jakarta was recorded in 1995, by which time the Ailsas were between 10 and 14 years old — and looking somewhat battle-scarred. *Richard Stedall*

The Citybus arrives

The Ailsa was not a sophisticated bus. Having the engine at the front, inside the passenger compartment, made it noisy. The driver's compartment was cramped. And the use of conventional leaf-spring suspension on most Ailsas meant that at the start of the 1980s the model's ride quality did not match that of a new generation of double-deckers designed from the outset with air suspension — the MCW Metrobus, Dennis Dominator, Scania BR112 and Leyland Titan and Olympian.

Ailsa sales volumes had been steady rather than spectacular in the UK. Home-market deliveries peaked at 145 in 1976, thanks to large orders from the South Yorkshire and West Midlands PTEs and from Tayside Regional Transport, but from 1977 to 1981 deliveries averaged just 56 vehicles a year, representing a share of less than 3% of the UK double-deck bus market.

For Volvo, a global manufacturer of cars, trucks and buses, the Ailsa was not a key model; indeed, its future was reviewed more than once. It was expensive to produce because of its low sales, and in reality its only Volvo parts were the engine and the electrics.

In terms of bus and coach chassis Volvo's real strength in the 1970s had been the mid-engined B58, a phenomenally successful model sold to operators around the world. This had been replaced in 1980 by the even more successful B10M, and it was this which would form the basis of a new Volvo double-decker, the Ailsa Citybus. This featured a perimeter chassis frame, which was the Ailsa's strongest feature, but with the B10M drivetrain — engine, gearbox and axles. These were shipped as kits from Sweden for incorporation into frames completed at Irvine. The frame was similar in concept to that of the Ailsa but without the central spine, impractical in a mid-engined

The first commercially produced underfloor-engined double-decker for service in Britain was this Strathclyde PTE Ailsa-badged Citybus, which took to the streets of Glasgow in the spring of 1982. It had an 86-seat Marshall body and was given an AH-series fleet number, indicating 'Ailsa Horizontal'. This photograph was taken in May, when the bus was just a few weeks old. It was the only X-registered Citybus. Stewart J. Brown

Proof that an underfloor-engined double-decker can negotiate a 14ft 6in high bridge, as Strathclyde's prototype Citybus passes under the Forth & Clyde Canal at Maryhill, in northwest Glasgow. Stewart J. Brown

Three more Citybuses with Marshall bodies were completed in the summer of 1983 for Derby City Transport, which was running 17 front-engined Ailsas. They were similar to the Strathclyde bus but had 78 seats and flat-glass windscreens. This one, with an Ailsa badge, is seen when new at a rally in Cardiff. Stewart J. Brown

The first Citybus demonstrator was bodied by East Lancs and entered service in the autumn of 1983. It is seen here in the summer of 1984 being tried by Colchester Borough Transport. The lettering on the side promotes the bus industry trade association, the Bus & Coach Council, and includes the slogan 'The New Approach To Public Transport'. Geoff Mills

In 1985 the original Citybus demonstrator was sold to A1 Service, being seen here in Irvine in March of that year. It passed to Stagecoach in 1995. Tony Wilson

chassis. It had instead two conventional parallel full-length frame members. The Citybus had air suspension as standard, with two bellows on the front axle and four at the rear, mounted on an H-frame.

Volvo publicity of the time commented: 'The chassis concept is a development of the well-tried Ailsa B55 philosophy, where engine positioning and simple driveline configuration combine to provide a simple-to-operate and cheap-to-maintain bus.'

The idea of building a double-deck body on the B10M was not immediately accepted by Volvo in Sweden, which suggested the rear-engined B10R might be more suitable. However, Volvo's UK management was aware that the B10R's reputation with mainland European operators was not of the best, and stuck with the B10M. To criticisms that engine access might be difficult there was a straightforward response: why is access important to an engine which never goes wrong?

The idea of an underfloor-engined double-decker was not new. AEC had built a prototype in 1950, the Regent IV, but this offered no significant benefits over the established front-engined Regent III and was not developed. In 1961 BMMO built two mid-engined D10 prototypes, one a front-entrance 78-seater, the other a dual-door bus with 65 seats; both buses operated for Midland Red until the start of the 1970s, but the company stuck with its front-engined D9.

So the Citybus revived an earlier concept, and showed that it could work. For Volvo the big benefit was that the Citybus was a spin-off from a successful high-volume chassis, unlike the Ailsa, which used a lot of unique componentry. For fleet engineers the Citybus still offered a simpler drivetrain than rear-engined models, as well as a high level of reliability. For operators' traffic departments the Citybus retained the high seating capacity of the Ailsa, or even improved on it. Ailsas typically seated 79 — or even 81 — while the Citybus could carry up to 84. By comparison a Dennis Dominator or Leyland Olympian usually had around 75 seats.

The downside of the Citybus was its high floor. Rear-engined double-deckers of the early 1980s normally had an entrance with two shallow steps. The Ailsa also had a two-step entrance. The Citybus had a three-step entrance. Access to public transport for disabled people was becoming an issue, but was not yet an over-riding consideration for either bus operators or bus makers. The Citybus was fitted with low-profile tyres to minimise the frame height.

Volvo approached Alexander and Northern Counties as potential builders of bodywork on the Citybus, but neither viewed it as a high priority, so the first Citybus had an 86-seat Marshall body. It entered service with Strathclyde PTE in the spring of 1982. The body featured an inter-deck floor made of a honeycomb material, developed from Marshall's experience in the aircraft industry. This was compact (helping to reduce overall height) and light (ensuring the Citybus met the requirements of the tilt test, which was a measure of the vehicle's stability). Cambridge-based Marshall had only started building double-deckers at the end of 1980 and was therefore not a significant force in that sector of

Towards the end of 1983 Nottingham City Transport took its first two Citybuses, and these had East Lancs bodywork to the operator's distinctive style, which included BET style double-curvature windscreens on both decks. They also had bonded glazing.
Royston Morgan

Half of the 30 Citybuses delivered in 1984 went to Derby City Transport. The first five were bodied by East Lancs and seated 76. As was often the way with East Lancs bodies of the time, the result was workmanlike rather than stylish, in this case with a particularly bland front end. They were followed by 10 more Marshall-bodied buses. *Stewart J. Brown*

The 10 Marshall-bodied Citybuses delivered to Derby in 1984 had a slightly revised body style with a simple front grille and deeper windscreens on the upper deck; 78-seaters, they were the last double-deckers built by Marshall. One leaves the city's bus station in 1989. *Geoff Mills*

the bus business. The initial drawings for the Marshall-bodied Citybus showed it being 14ft 9in high; the novel inter-deck floor brought that down to 14ft 7in.

A 9.6-litre Volvo THD100 engine was fitted — this was the standard B10M engine, but downrated to 162bhp and driving through an SCG gearbox. On production models the standard power rating was 210bhp, with 245 and 276bhp options. These were comfortably within the THD100's operational parameters; on coaches it was offered with an even higher 310bhp rating.

The SCG gearbox was just one of three choices and proved to be the least popular. Most operators went for either ZF or Voith transmission, both of which incorporated an integral retarder. A Ferodo retarder was available with the SCG gearbox.

Two wheelbases were offered on the Citybus — 4,953mm for a nominal overall length of 9.5 or 10.1m, and 5,639mm for a nominal 11.1m overall length. The wheelbase was indicated as a suffix to the chassis code — B10M-50 or B10M-56. Most Citybus buyers specified the shorter wheelbase. The gross vehicle weight was 16.5 tonnes. While the model was initially promoted as the Ailsa Citybus, it was soon rebranded as a Volvo. The chassis designation also changed from time to time, the model being described variously as the D10M and the B10MD — the 'D' in both cases indicating a double-decker.

A three-axle variant, based on the B10MT coach chassis, was considered, but none was built.

Benefits of the Citybus, apart from high seating capacity, included a flat floor with minimum wheel-arch intrusion, good weight distribution and relatively low unladen weight. Weight comparisons are difficult, but, as an example, a typical SBG Alexander-bodied Citybus weighed around 9.4 tonnes unladen, which was 400kg lighter than an equivalent Leyland Olympian. And on top of all that it was reliable.

The chassis for the Strathclyde bus was a Swedish-built B10M modified at Volvo's Irvine plant, as were the next three chassis, which were also bodied by Marshall and entered service with

Derby City Transport in the summer of 1983. Derby was, of course, an existing Ailsa user, with 17 in service. Derby had an SCG gearbox in one of its Citybuses and ZFs in the other two. A ZF gearbox was later fitted to the SCG-equipped bus.

In the autumn of 1983 a Citybus demonstrator, A308 RSU, was built for Volvo. This had an 83-seat East Lancs body, and was later sold to A1 Service. In addition two Citybuses were delivered to Nottingham City Transport, a new customer for Volvo. They had 88-seat East Lancs bodies to that operator's distinctive style. Nottingham would become a major Citybus user, building up a fleet of 48.

There was no question that the concept worked, but sales volumes were low in the mid-1980s, averaging just over 30 a year — significantly fewer than the Ailsa's annual average of 56. This in part reflected changes in the funding of new buses, the Government having phased out a capital grant of 50% of the purchase price. New Bus Grant, as it was known, had boosted sales in the 1970s. There was also growing uncertainty about the future of the bus industry, with both privatisation and deregulation looming. Deregulation dramatically depressed the demand for big

Derby's final Citybuses were bodied by Northern Counties. As built (left), the 1986 vehicles featured a very plain front panel, but this was replaced by a much more attractive design (below) before the buses entered service.
Gerald Truran,
Stewart J. Brown

With its Ailsa grille and cab door this looks for all the world like an Ailsa — but is in fact a Citybus. Tayside took five East Lancs-bodied examples in 1984, three of which were 89-seat buses. Although they had the engine under the floor rather than at the front, there was little difference externally between the 1984 Citybuses and the East Lancs-bodied Ailsas delivered the previous year. *Donald MacRae*

Two of the Citybuses delivered to Tayside in 1984 were fitted with East Lancs coach bodies. They were named after local rivers, the Tay and the Tummel. Here the newly delivered *River Tay* arrives at the coast in Blackpool. *Stewart J. Brown*

buses in the latter part of the 1980s. Conversely, privatisation opened doors for Volvo, as privatised former NBC operators no longer felt obliged to buy Leylands.

In 1984 the biggest Citybus buyer was Derby, which took another 15 — 10 more with Marshall bodies and five bodied by East Lancs. Derby would place two more orders for Citybuses, taking a further five in 1986 and its last five in 1988. These two batches were bodied by Northern Counties. For the month of November 1985 Derby City Transport's Chief Engineer, Gerald Truran, reported fuel consumption of

6.12mpg for his fleet's Citybuses, compared with 6.41 for Ailsas — but with the qualification that the Citybuses more typically returned 6.4mpg, on a par with the fleet's Ailsas.

Tayside, which by 1983 had bought 161 Ailsas, took its first Citybuses in 1984, five with bodies by East Lancs. Three were 89-seat buses and, unusually for East Lancs-bodied Citybuses, incorporated Ailsa-style grilles. The other two were 78-seat coaches.

Having taken the prototype Citybus in 1982, Strathclyde PTE took a further five in 1984. These were the first Citybuses to be bodied by Alexander, the company which had supplied the bodywork on the vast majority of Ailsas, and had Ailsa-style grilles. They were unusual in that a wheelchair lift was incorporated in the front entrance; Strathclyde was something of a pioneer in making buses accessible to wheelchair users. In the forward area of the lower saloon there were longitudinal tip-up seats — novel at the time, although destined to become commonplace — to provide space for wheelchairs. One of the buses was exhibited at the 1983 Scottish Motor Show. At this time Strathclyde was, of course, still buying Ailsas (as well as Leyland Olympians and MCW Metrobuses).

At the other end of Britain, Plymouth Citybus took two Citybus coaches, with 78-seat East Lancs bodies. Similar vehicles would be supplied to a small number of other fleets.

The first Citybuses for the Scottish Bus Group were two delivered to Fife at the end of 1984 in place of two cancelled Ailsas. These were 11.7m long and had stylish Alexander RVC coach

Plymouth Citybus was an early customer for the Citybus, taking two with 78-seat East Lancs coach bodies in 1984. This one, named *Ark Royal* in recognition of the city's naval heritage, is seen in the city centre in 1985 (left). Both coaches were later fitted with 79 bus seats and with BET-style windscreens in place of the deep — and expensive to replace — screens which were part of the East Lancs coach design. Mark Bailey

bodies with 70 seats. The RVC was based on Alexander's R-type body and had bonded glazing, luggage racks and a plug door, and was described in Alexander's brochure as 'a study in solid reliable engineering combined with modern elegance'. One was exhibited by Alexander at the 1984 Motor Show. At first they operated in Citylink colours on the service between Edinburgh and Perth, but by the end of 1985 they had been repainted in Fife coach livery. In 1987 they were transferred to Western,

for use on the Ayr–Glasgow service. Only two RVC bodies were built, along with two broadly similar RLC bodies on Leyland Olympian chassis for Eastern Scottish. Clearly reliable engineering and modern elegance weren't its greatest selling points.

There were only two export Citybuses. The first, a 10m bus with a 91-seat dual-door Alexander R-type body, was delivered to Kowloon Motor Bus in Hong Kong in mid-1984. It was not badged as a Citybus — this being the trading name of one of KMB's competitors — but instead carried a B10MD badge on the grille. It ran for only four years, being destroyed by a fire in 1988. The second was an 11m-long dual-door East Lancs-bodied demonstrator supplied to Singapore Bus Service. Like the Ailsa demonstrator three years before, it failed to produce any orders.

Further Citybuses for Fife were delivered in the early months of 1985, but this time with conventional 84-seat Alexander R-type bodies. They were soon followed by five similar vehicles for sister SBG operator Eastern. Both companies were existing Ailsa operators.

The biggest 1985 Citybus delivery was to Nottingham, which took 14. The body order was divided equally between East Lancs and Northern Counties. All were dual-door buses bodied to Nottingham's own design, with 84 seats in the Northern Counties bodies and 86 seats in those built by East Lancs — an unusually high figure for a dual-door bus. The seven with Northern Counties bodywork were the first Citybuses to be bodied by the Wigan builder, preceding those for Derby. In fact, in marked contrast to the Ailsa — of which 78% of those supplied to British operators had Alexander bodywork — the Citybus was bodied in significant numbers by both East Lancs (127) and Northern Counties (109). Marshall bodied just 14 — but the company had never really been a significant supplier of double-deck bodies. All of which left 337 — 57% — with Alexander bodies.

Members of the A1 Service co-operative had been steady buyers of Ailsas, taking 11 new examples between 1976 and 1979. However, the withdrawal of New Bus Grant saw a decline in the purchase of new buses by small operators, and only two new Citybuses were delivered to A1. These had Alexander bodies and entered service in 1985. In the same year one other small business — Wrights of Wrexham — bought a new Citybus; this had a 78-seat East Lancs coach body. Volvo also built a second demonstrator, B108 CCS, with Alexander bodywork to an A1-style specification, which was tried by a number of operators from March 1985 before being sold, to Fife, in 1986.

The most interesting of 1985's Citybus deliveries was a one-off for London Buses. The first underfloor-engined double-decker for London would have been an event in itself, but the Citybus was particularly unusual in being fitted with hydraulic accumulators. This system, promoted by Volvo as Cumulo, harnessed energy which would otherwise be lost during braking and turned it back into motive power using compressed nitrogen. As the bus pulled away from a stop the stored power was released, and the Volvo THD100 diesel engine then ran at idling speed until the accumulators were exhausted. The system was heavy — it added 750kg to the unladen weight of the Citybus — but was designed to reduce fuel consumption, Volvo claiming savings of up to 30%. The bus had a dual-door Alexander body, with a split-step entrance. Exhibited at the May 1985 UITP Congress in Brussels, it operated in London for just over 12 months from the middle of 1986, mainly on route 102 from Palmers Green garage. However, the trial was not a success, and the bus was returned to Volvo in September 1987, whereupon it was rebuilt with a standard Citybus driveline featuring a ZF gearbox before being sold to A1. It later joined the fleet of Black Prince, of Leeds.

Greater Manchester PTE was always ready to evaluate new types of bus, and had taken three Ailsas in the early 1980s. In 1986 three Citybuses joined the PTE fleet. These had 79-seat Northern Counties bodies and were based at Wigan, which was also home to the PTE's three Ailsas.

There were two new municipal customers for the Citybus in 1986, Bournemouth and Northampton, the former taking five with 76-seat East Lancs coach bodies; it would buy 10 more Citybuses in 1988/9, but with 80-seat Alexander R-type bus bodies. Both operators had previously been Leyland customers, and their switch to Volvo was indicative of how the Citybus, helped by a changing political climate, was securing new business for Volvo at Leyland's expense, in a way that the Ailsa had not.

The Scottish Bus Group's first Citybuses were two long-wheelbase chassis fitted with dramatic Alexander RVC bodies. They entered traffic with Fife Scottish on the service between Perth and Edinburgh at the end of 1984. Only two bodies of this style were built, along with two broadly similar RLC bodies on Leyland Olympian chassis for Eastern Scottish.
Stewart J. Brown

The Kowloon Motor Bus Co took one Alexander-bodied Citybus for evaluation. A dual-door 91-seater, it entered service in 1984 and is seen here in October of that year. It operated for only four years, being destroyed by fire in 1988. Note the B10MD badge.
C. W. Davison

Northampton became a major Citybus user, starting off with two, with 76-seat East Lancs coach bodies, in 1986. Then came a break, but in 1989 it commenced a programme of buying six Citybuses a year, concluded four years later. Thus by the end of 1993 Northampton was running 32 Citybuses, all but two of which had Alexander bodywork with 82 high-backed coach seats.

The immediate aftermath of bus deregulation in 1986 saw a dearth of new orders for big buses, and this was reflected in Citybus deliveries, which in 1987 hit a low of 27 vehicles. These included the last for SBG, which had ordered six for Western and four for Eastern, although two of those intended for Western were diverted to Fife, in exchange for the latter company's two 1985 Citybus/Alexander RVC coaches. One of the Western vehicles was exhibited at the 1987 Coach & Bus exhibition.

This turmoil in the bus industry prompted Volvo to reappraise Citybus production, which was being undertaken at Irvine, which had built the Ailsa. The decision was made that it would be more economic to build the chassis in the main B10M plant at Borås, in Sweden. In effect this meant supplying standard chassis to the bodybuilders, which would then fit the perimeter frame. Officially, the Citybus name was dropped — but nobody outside Volvo took much notice.

Great Yarmouth Transport, which had last purchased new double-deck buses — Bristol VRTs — in 1981, took two Citybuses in 1987, and these had East Lancs 78-seat coach bodies.

They would be followed in 1989 by two more Citybuses, but with Alexander bus bodywork; these were Volvo stock vehicles.

Another new customer for the Citybus in 1987 was London coach operator Grey-Green, which received two with coach-seated Alexander RV bodies for operation on Kent commuter services. They were 78-seaters and fitted comfortably in a fleet running B10M coaches. Also bodied by Alexander in 1987, but as a standard bus, was the third and final Citybus demonstrator, registered E825 OMS by the bodybuilder. It was later sold to Nottingham City Transport.

Illustrative of the new markets being opened up to Volvo and other European manufacturers was the biggest Citybus delivery of 1987, comprising 12 vehicles for recently privatised Badgerline — formerly part of NBC and with a fleet consisting mainly of Bristols and Leylands. The Citybuses had Alexander bodywork and were part of a larger order which included B10M buses with Alexander P-type bodies and B10M/Van Hool coaches. As part of the deal Volvo provided contract maintenance for the new fleet — a novel step at the time and still relatively uncommon two decades later.

Another ex-NBC company to buy Alexander-bodied Citybuses was Western National, which took three in 1988. These were part of a batch of five vehicles built for Volvo stock, the other two being purchased by Filers of Ilfracombe and Whippet of Fenstanton. Whippet would go on to buy three Northern Counties-bodied Citybuses in 1989/90.

Above: Fife Scottish operated Ailsas, so the move to Citybuses came as no great surprise. Delivered in 1985 were eight with Alexander RV bodywork, among them this one claiming to be 'Best Bus Around' — a message undermined somewhat by a replacement panel which means that part of the letter 'd' is missing. Stewart J. Brown

Left: The first Citybuses for Eastern Scottish in 1985 looked similar to the company's later Ailsas, as comparison with the photograph on page 31 will show. Like the Fife bus pictured above, this vehicle, seen in Edinburgh in 1987, has an incomplete 'Best Bus' message on the side. Tony Wilson

Below: In 1985 Nottingham City Transport added 14 Citybuses to its fleet. The first seven had 86-seat dual-door bodywork by East Lancs, being broadly similar to the first two buses delivered in November 1983 but with the addition of a deep glazed sliding door for the driver. Stewart J. Brown

The Northern Counties-bodied buses were similar in concept but with gasket glazing and a Volvo-style grille. The nearside view (left) shows the narrow entrance door favoured by Nottingham. The offside view (below) shows the inward-facing seat on the upper deck above the driver and dates from 1998, by which time Nottingham had adopted a brighter livery with a lighter shade of green and more cream relief.
Stewart J. Brown collection, Peter Rowlands

Two new Citybuses were
delivered to A1 in 1985,
both with Alexander bodies.
This bus, seen in Irvine in
1991, carried registration
TSD 285 from new,
the number having been
transferred from a 1962
Leyland Titan PD3.
Peter Rowlands

The second of three Citybus
demonstrators was an
Alexander-bodied bus
which was used by Volvo in
1985/6. Here it is running
for Wright of Wrexham,
on the service to Penycae.
It was later sold to Fife
Scottish. John Robinson

Wright did buy a Citybus, with an East Lancs coach body which featured windscreen wipers for the upper-deck passengers.
Tony Wilson

London's Citybus with the Cumulo drive system had a short life in the capital, and was based at Palmers Green garage for use mainly on route 102, which ran between Golders Green and Chingford. The split-step entrance was designed to improve access for people with restricted mobility, while the yellow entrance doors were supposed to aid people with impaired vision.
Tony Wilson

The Cumulo bus was quickly fitted with a conventional drivetrain and after a period in Scotland with A1 was purchased by Black Prince of Leeds. Andrew Jarosz

Three Citybuses joined the three Ailsas in the Greater Manchester PTE fleet at Wigan in 1986 and, like the Ailsas, had Northern Counties bodies. This one displays the short-lived GM Buses fleetname and a coloured strip between the wheel-arches denoting allocation to the western area of the PTE's new commercial company. Stewart J. Brown

56

The last new double-deckers for Western Scottish while it was part of the Scottish Bus Group were six Citybuses delivered at the end of 1987, by which time Alexander had replaced the Volvo radiator grille with a more subtle front panel of its own design. These vehicles had coach seats and at various times in their lives wore different versions of Western's black, white, grey and red livery.
Stewart J. Brown

The final Citybuses for the Scottish Bus Group were delivered in 1987 and included four for Eastern Scottish with coach-seated Alexander RV-type bodies. This photograph was taken in Edinburgh in 1989.
Tony Wilson

The two Citybuses delivered to Great Yarmouth in the summer of 1987 had East Lancs bodywork with 78 coach seats. They are seen here on a private hire at Pleasurewood Hills American theme park in Lowestoft, which destination has been programmed into the dot-matrix destination display. Note also the centrally-located emergency exit. Geoff Mills

Two more Citybuses joined the Great Yarmouth fleet in 1989. These had Alexander RV bodies with Volvo B10M badging below the windscreen. Geoff Mills

For Kent commuter services Grey-Green took two Citybuses with 78-seat Alexander bodies in 1987. Between the morning and evening peaks they were used on sightseeing work in Central London; here one makes a spirited exit from Whitehall in the summer of 1988. Peter Rowlands

The final Citybus demonstrator was commissioned in 1987 and had an Alexander body. It is seen here operating for Plymouth Citybus in March 1988. Mark Bailey

The 1987 demonstrator differed from the previous (1985) Alexander-bodied demonstrator in having flat-glass windscreens and Alexander's own front panel in place of the Ailsa-style grille. It was eventually sold to Nottingham City Transport, which operated it until 2004. Peter Rowlands

The first former National Bus Company subsidiary to buy Citybuses was Badgerline, which introduced 12 to its Weston-super-Mare depot in 1987 in a deal which included B10M buses and coaches, with contract maintenance supplied by **Volvo.** Stewart J. Brown

Western National was another former NBC company to buy Citybuses, taking three stock vehicles in March 1988. These had Alexander R-type bodies with 82 coach seats. This one is seen in Plymouth in October 1988, on the express service to Torquay. Mark Bailey

The sole new double-deck for Filer's of Ilfracombe was this Citybus, an Alexander-bodied stock vehicle, which was purchased in 1988. It is seen here in Bideford in 1990. A B10M badge is fitted above the front offside wheel, adjacent to the side trafficator. Mark Bailey

Above left: **Whippet of Fenstanton used a distinctive livery, as demonstrated by its first Citybus, a stock-build Alexander-bodied vehicle delivered in 1988. It is seen in Cambridge in 2000.** Mark Bailey

Left: **Whippet bought another three Citybuses — two in 1989 and one in 1990 — but for these specified Northern Counties bodywork. This is the last of the three, looking immaculate when photographed in Cambridge, despite being 10 years old.** Mark Bailey

Above: **Bournemouth took another five Citybuses — this time with Alexander bodywork rather than East Lancs — in 1988 and followed these with five more identical vehicles in 1989. Note the comprehensive destination display on this 1989 bus.** Peter Rowlands

The London influence

Citybus deliveries in the late 1980s were boosted by repeat business from Nottingham, which took 15 buses in 1988 and a further five in 1989, but the most significant order to date came from an unlikely source. Grey-Green had become involved in local bus operation in the capital in 1987 after London Regional Transport started its programme of route tendering, securing a few suburban contracts, generally operated by second-hand double-deckers. But in 1988 it became the first independent to win a tender in the heart of London when it was awarded the 24 (Pimlico–Hampstead Heath), a route which ran through Parliament Square, Whitehall and Trafalgar Square. For this high-profile service it bought 30 new Alexander-bodied Citybuses at a cost of £2.5 million, or around £83,000 per vehicle — the biggest Citybus order yet placed. The 75-seat Citybuses had 245bhp engines, making them at the time the most powerful double-deckers to have operated on local services in London. The choice of the Citybus was a logical one for Grey-Green, which was already running a fleet of Volvo B10M coaches, in addition to its existing pair of coach-seated Citybuses in use on Kent commuter services.

Grey-Green specified split-level entrance steps to ease boarding, although passengers were still confronted with a precipitous three-step centre exit when it came to getting off. The Citybuses introduced a distinctive new livery by Best Impressions using, appropriately, grey and green relieved by an orange band which reflected the Orange Luxury business, which had been part of the Ewer Group, former owner of Grey-Green.

Smaller orders saw the delivery in 1988 of four East Lancs-bodied Citybuses to Lincoln City Transport — that operator's last new double-deckers — and two to Burnley & Pendle Transport. The Burnley & Pendle buses had Alexander RV bodies with coach seats; a further 10 followed in 1989 but with bus seats. The Lincoln vehicles were allocated KIB-series Ulster registrations from new — an unusual example of a municipally-owned operator choosing registrations which hid the vehicles' age.

In 1988 Boro'line Maidstone was struggling to secure the delivery of new buses from Optare for operation on LRT contracts in the Bexley area, and to help cover the shortfall took one Alexander-bodied Citybus from Volvo. This vehicle had been an exhibit at the 1987 Coach & Bus show at the NEC. The municipally-owned company then secured the LRT tender for service 188, which operated from Greenwich to Euston, and for this it ordered 14 Alexander-bodied Citybuses, broadly similar to those running for Grey-Green; these entered service in the early part of 1989. When Boro'line collapsed in 1992 the company's 15 Citybuses were among the vehicles acquired by Kentish Bus, which took over Boro'line's LRT contracts.

In fact, 1989 was to be the best year for the Citybus, almost 240 being delivered, representing an incredible 40% of all Citybus sales. The biggest customer was PTE-owned Strathclyde Buses, which took the bulk of an order for 95 Citybuses with Alexander bodies, the balance following in 1990. These, added to six purchased in the early 1980s, took the Strathclyde Citybus fleet to 101, the country's biggest by a handsome margin. Scotland's biggest Ailsa operator, Tayside, took 15 Citybuses — its last — in 1989; these had 84-seat Alexander bodies. New bus purchases at Tayside in the 1990s would be single-deckers.

In London, Grey-Green and Boro'line Maidstone were running Citybuses on LRT contracts, and part of the 1989 sales boom was down to London operators. London General took 27 with Northern Counties bodywork for route 133 (Tooting Broadway–Liverpool Street). They were based at Stockwell garage, as were a further 12 similar buses delivered in 1990/1 for the 196 (Norwood Junction–Brixton). All were of dual-door layout. At the time of their delivery they were the heaviest vehicles in the London Buses fleet, weighing 10,465kg; by comparison a London Olympian/ECW turned the scales at 9,718kg. However, the Citybuses were 80-seaters, compared with just 68 seats in an Olympian.

Another London-area operator, Drawlane subsidiary London & Country, took 38 Citybuses in 1989, primarily for a range of LRT contracts in outer South West London and Surrey. These were single-door buses — 25 with 80-seat bodies by Northern Counties and 13 with 88-seat bodies by East Lancs. The high capacity of the East Lancs bodies was achieved by means of an extended rear overhang; all 38 vehicles were based on the standard-wheelbase B10M-50 chassis. They wore a stylish livery — another Best Impressions creation — of two-tone green with a red band, signifying the link between the company's original outer-London operations and its growing presence in traditional 'red bus' territory. The Northern Counties Citybuses were licensed to carry 19 standing passengers, giving a total capacity of 99.

Away from London, Drawlane took a further 14 East Lancs-bodied Citybuses for its North Western business. These were similar to the London & Country vehicles, and 10 would later head south to join two Drawlane London-area fleets, Londonlinks and Kentish Bus.

The Drawlane companies buying Citybuses were all former NBC subsidiaries, and two other ex-NBC companies bought Citybuses in 1989. Trent took 24 with Alexander bodies as it embarked on a major programme of investment in new vehicles. However, these were to be the company's last new double-deckers. All subsequent purchases would be single-deck, Trent opting to provide more frequent services, rather than run bigger buses.

The other ex-NBC customer was Southdown, which took 12 Northern Counties-bodied Citybuses. These were the only new double-deckers bought by the company during its brief period as an independent operator and were delivered in a variant of the company's traditional pre-NBC livery of apple green and cream. The Citybuses were delivered in June and July; the company was bought by Stagecoach in August. Inevitably the attractive Southdown green succumbed to Stagecoach's brash corporate livery of white with multi-coloured stripes.

A further batch of stock vehicles was built in 1989, this time 10, again bodied by Alexander. Four were purchased by Nottingham City Transport, and two, as described earlier, by Great Yarmouth. Three independents —

Nottingham's 1988 East Lancs-bodied Citybuses used the same basic structure as earlier deliveries but with gasket rather than bonded glazing. They also dispensed with a separate door for the driver. There were 15 buses in the batch, which were delivered in the operator's traditional livery of dark green and cream. Note the single-piece entrance door and substantial bumper. The offside view dates from the 1990s, by which time the livery had been revised. Stewart J. Brown collection, Stewart J. Brown

Crawford of Neilston, Finglands of Manchester and Dewhirst of Bradford — bought one each, while the final vehicle went to the Hanley Crouch Community Association in North London, where it replaced an 11-year-old Ailsa. Crawford's Citybus was bought for use on an express service between Glasgow and Ardrossan. The Finglands vehicle was the company's first new double-decker and was used on local services in south Manchester, where it ran alongside assorted second-hand Fleetlines and Metrobuses. Dewhirst used its Citybus for private hires.

After the peak of 1989, Citybus sales dropped rapidly. The most significant deliveries of 1990 were repeat orders from two London operators. London & Country took a further 36 with East Lancs bodywork, this time dual-door, for operation on two routes in Central London, the 78 (Shoreditch–Forest Hill) and 176 (Oxford Circus–Penge); these were delivered in the winter of 1990/1. And there were 14 more Alexander-bodied Citybuses for Grey-Green. Eight were dual-door buses, in part to cover LRT route 168 (Hampstead Heath–Elephant & Castle), while six were single-door, primarily for the suburban 173 (Stratford–Becontree Heath).

As well as buying new Citybuses, Grey-Green created what might be regarded as quasi-Citybuses by having nine Volvo B10M coaches rebodied as double-deckers in 1991. The new bodies were built by East Lancs but were a straight copy of the Alexander RV. The rebodied B10Ms were, however, immediately distinguishable from genuine Citybuses by their long wheelbase — 6.1m against 5.0m on a

When Grey-Green secured the London Regional Transport contract for route 24 between Hampstead Heath and Pimlico it ordered Volvo Citybuses for this high-profile service. The initial order was for 30, delivered in the autumn of 1988. Two are seen at Pimlico soon after entering service. Geoff Mills

The last new double-deckers for Lincoln City Transport were four Citybuses with 79-seat East Lancs coach bodywork. They were delivered in 1988 and had dateless Ulster registrations from new. The dot-matrix destination display was something of a novelty at the time. Mark Bailey

Burnley & Pendle's first new double-deckers for 10 years were two Citybuses which were delivered in 1988. They were followed by 10 more in 1989, one of which is seen in Burnley bus station. They had Alexander bodies. Gavin Booth

standard Citybus — and their unusually short rear overhang. They were used initially on route 141 (Wood Green–Moorgate).

One of the reasons for the fall in Citybus sales was that in 1988 Volvo had purchased Leyland Bus. This gave Volvo a rear-engined double-decker, the Olympian, and if it didn't quite render the Citybus surplus to requirements, it certainly meant that Volvo no longer needed it to secure double-deck bus sales. Production of the Olympian at the Leyland factory in Workington ceased in 1993, whereupon the model was rebadged as a Volvo, offered with a Volvo engine and built at Volvo's Irvine factory, where it reintroduced the manufacture of double-deck chassis after a five-year break.

So the Citybus was on its way out. Deliveries in 1991 included the completion of batches for London General and London & Country, along with the first eight of a 10-bus order for Greater Manchester Buses, the final two — which had wheelchair lifts incorporated in the entrance, as tried by Strathclyde in 1984 — following in 1992. There were also three more Alexander-bodied buses for Burnley & Pendle, taking its Citybus fleet to 15. Plymouth Citybus, which had been an early Citybus buyer with two East Lancs-bodied coaches in 1984, took two more in 1991. When new they lacked destination displays and operated in the Plymouth CityCoach fleet; a single-line dot-matrix display was added later. Two further batches of Alexander-bodied buses for Northampton entered service in 1992/3. And most people assumed that was the end of the Citybus.

But not quite. In 1997, Nottingham City Transport, which had in service 37 Citybuses — 36 bought new, plus an ex-demonstrator — took delivery of a further 10, all bodied by East Lancs. Five were 82-seat coaches; the other five were 84-seat buses. These buses, with their three-step entrances, were placed in service in November, at the same time as the first examples of a new generation of step-free low-entry double-deckers were being exhibited at the 1997 Coach & Bus event at the National Exhibition Centre.

East Lancs was called upon to build another body for a Citybus in 1998, rebodying one of Northampton's 1992 buses which had been damaged in an accident. It was fitted with a Pyoneer body, similar to those on the 1997 Nottingham vehicles. It seated 78, with four fewer seats in the lower saloon than in the original Alexander RV body.

Yet even that was not the end. One more Citybus — the last — was built for Nottingham in 2002. This, with an 02 registration, had an East Lancs coach body and bore Nottingham City Coaches fleetnames. It was the last step-entrance double-decker to enter service in Britain. And it had a short life with Nottingham, being sold in 2005.

The Citybus was bought new by 32 British operators, compared with 20 buyers of new Ailsas. Of the 20 Ailsa buyers, nine — A1, Derby, Eastern Scottish, Fife Scottish, Greater Manchester, Hanley Crouch, Tayside, Strathclyde and Western Scottish — also bought Citybuses. (London Buses is excluded from this list, its only Citybus being the trial Cumulo bus, never regarded as a permanent addition to the fleet.)

Late delivery of Optare-bodied Leyland Olympians saw Boro'line Maidstone cancel two outstanding vehicles, replacing them with two stock Scanias, plus a Citybus which it purchased from Volvo. It entered service still in Volvo's demonstration livery and carrying the registration intended for one of the cancelled Olympians. Stewart J. Brown

Boro'line secured a number of London Regional Transport contracts, including that for route 188 (Euston Station–Greenwich). Boro'line had a stylish livery, designed by the Best Impressions consultancy, with route branding which included the number 188 alongside the fleetname, and a route diagram below the side windows towards the rear. To operate the service the company took 14 Alexander-bodied Citybuses, one of which is seen here on Waterloo Bridge. The bus originally had opening sections in both front upper-deck windows. Peter Rowlands

In 1989/90 Strathclyde
Buses received a major
intake of Citybuses,
comprising no fewer than
95 with Alexander RV
bodies. By the end of 1990
Strathclyde was running
Britain's biggest fleet of
Citybuses, with 101.
Alexander had restyled
the front panel, improving
the body's appearance.
Stewart J. Brown

Tayside's last Citybuses
were 15 delivered in 1989,
which saw Alexander
supplying bodies after an
eight-year gap. Unusually,
these had offside cab doors,
a feature specified on
Citybuses only by Tayside
and Nottingham City
Transport. The rubber-
mounted front upper-deck
windows were peculiar to
Tayside. Donald MacRae

London General took 39 Citybuses with dual-door Northern Counties bodies in the period 1989-91. One heads south at Streatham Hill on its way from Liverpool Street Station to Tooting Broadway in the summer of 1991. Note the split-step entrance. Tony Wilson

In 1989 London & Country bought 25 Citybuses with Northern Counties bodies, primarily for use on London Regional Transport contracted services, although they were also used on other routes, as shown by this 1990 view of one on the service from Croydon to Godstone. These buses were licensed to carry 99 passengers. Peter Rowlands

London & Country also took 13 East Lancs-bodied Citybuses, with an extended rear overhang. These single-door buses seated 88 and were allocated initially to LRT contracts in Southwest London. Gavin Booth

North Western was, like London & Country, part of the Drawlane group and also received Citybuses with extra-long East Lancs 88-seat bodies. There were 14 such vehicles in the fleet, delivered in the winter of 1989/90. This one is seen on an excursion in Fleetwood in the summer of 1995. Mark Bailey

Trent's last new double-deck buses were 24 Citybuses with Alexander bodywork, delivered in 1989. They were the only new double-deckers bought by the company after it was privatised, and joined a double-deck fleet made up mainly of NBC-era Bristol VRTs and Leyland Olympians. Peter Rowlands

The light green associated with Southdown in pre-NBC days was revived by the company's new owners when it was privatised in 1989. Twelve Citybuses were the only double-deckers delivered in this attractive livery, the company being sold to Stagecoach just weeks after they were delivered. They had Northern Counties bodywork with 76 high-backed coach seats and dot-matrix destination displays. Stewart J. Brown

Nottingham took five stock Alexander-bodied Citybuses in 1989. These were to the bodybuilder's standard layout — single door, 82 seats. Nottingham's own style of body could squeeze in up to 86 seats, and with two doors. Geoff Mills

A Volvo-stock Citybus was purchased by Finglands of Manchester. Fitted with coach seats, it was suitable for use as a private-hire vehicle — as here at Manchester's Piccadilly station — as well as operating on the company's local bus services. Delivered in 1989, it was Finglands' first new double-decker. The company would later buy similar used vehicles from Trent. Peter Rowlands

Dewhirst of Bradford was another buyer for the stock Citybuses built in 1989. Its vehicle was used for school contracts and private hires. Raised seating towards the rear of the lower deck was a feature of Alexander-bodied Citybuses and can be seen clearly in this view. Andrew Jarosz

Crawford of Neilston bought one Citybus, with an Alexander body, seen here leaving Glasgow's Buchanan Bus Station for Ardrossan. New in 1989, it was registered in Leicestershire by the dealer that supplied it, along with five B10M coaches — Yeates of Loughborough. Stewart J. Brown

In 1990 London & Country won two more London contracts, for which it bought a further 36 East Lancs-bodied Citybuses, this time standard-length dual-door models. The Central London services were for a period branded 'Londonlinks', as seen in this view in the Strand. This is bus 667; it should have been 666, but a matching registration was not available, the Driver & Vehicle Licensing Agency having decided not to issue what some called 'the devil's number' — a reference to the New Testament Book of Revelations.
Stewart J. Brown

As the focus of its business moved from coaches to buses, Grey-Green had nine Volvo B10M chassis rebodied as double-deckers by East Lancs in 1991, making them Citybus lookalikes. The give-away was the long wheelbase and short rear overhang. The body was a copy of the Alexander RV. This bus carries advertising for Cowie Interleasing — a sister company in the Cowie group. Peter Rowlands

GM Buses, 'arm's length' successor to Greater Manchester PTE's directly controlled bus operation, continued to evaluate different types of buses and in 1991 ordered 10 Citybuses, along with 10 Dennis Dominators and five Scanias. All were bodied by Northern Counties. When new the Citybuses were used on a Manchester–Bury rail-replacement service, pending the opening of the Metrolink tramway in April 1992; this bus has just crossed the as yet unused Metrolink tracks at Shudehill in central Manchester. Peter Rowlands

The two Citybus coaches delivered to Plymouth Citybus in 1991 had East Lancs coach bodies, but of a different style from the pair delivered in 1984, with a greater number of side windows. They were 78-seaters, with a rear luggage compartment, and when new had no destination displays. Mark Bailey

Northampton Transport took delivery of its last Citybuses — six with Alexander bodies — in the summer of 1993. Later that year the business was purchased by GRT Holdings, and this 1996 view features a 1992 bus in GRT's corporate livery. Tony Wilson

Above: Having suffered fire damage, one of Northampton's later Citybuses — the one illustrated in the previous photograph — was rebodied in 1998 with an East Lancs Pyoneer body and given a dateless WSU registration in place of its original K-prefix number. It is seen at that year's Showbus event in what was then First's corporate livery, which still retained a distinctive local identity but would soon be swept away by the so-called 'Barbie' scheme. Tony Wilson

The last significant batch of Citybuses entered service with Nottingham towards the end of 1997. These were the first Citybuses for five years, and there were 10, all bodied by East Lancs to the builder's Pyoneer design. Five were single-door 84-seat buses. Along with the Citybuses Nottingham took 15 Volvo Olympians, also with Pyoneer bodies. Peter Rowlands

One solitary Citybus was delivered to Nottingham in the summer of 2002, five years after what might reasonably have been thought to have been the last of the type. The East Lancs Pyoneer body was fitted with 82 coach seats, and the vehicle wore Nottingham City Coaches livery. Bob Gell

Leyland's response

The arrival of the Volvo Citybus prompted a response from Leyland, which turned to its Danish subsidiary, DAB, to supply underframes as the basis of a mid-engined double-decker, launched as the Lion. It attracted only two customers — the Scottish Bus Group and Nottingham City Transport — both of which were buying Citybuses.

The Lion, like the Citybus, had a perimeter frame. It was powered by Leyland's 11.1-litre TL11H engine, rated at 245bhp, driving through a ZF automatic gearbox with integral retarder. Designed for a nominal length of 10m, it had a wheelbase of 5,180mm.

The first 10, with Alexander R type bodywork, entered service with Eastern Scottish in the summer of 1986 and were soon followed by three, with Northern Counties bodies, for Nottingham. For 1987 SBG ordered a further nine — three for Eastern and six for Kelvin Scottish. The three Eastern vehicles entered service in the summer, but Kelvin was in financial difficulties and was unable to take delivery of its Lions. One was registered in June and was used by Leyland as a demonstrator before it, along with the other five, were delivered to Clydeside Scottish at the end of the year. The demonstrator failed to produce any orders.

No Lions entered service in 1988. The last were a further 10 for Nottingham, this time with East Lancs bodies, which entered service at the start of 1989.

So in the end Leyland sold only 32 of its Citybus lookalike over three years. It wasn't the company's greatest success.

Only the Scottish Bus Group and Nottingham City Transport bought Leyland Lions. The last 10, all bodied by East Lancs, entered service with Nottingham at the start of 1989 and comprised five 80-seat coaches and five 88-seat buses. The last of the Lions shows detail body differences from the 1988 Citybus illustrated on page 67, in particular the absence of glazing by the staircase and a less tidy treatment of the lower-deck emergency door.
Peter Rowlands

The first Lions in Scotland were three for Eastern Scottish, which entered service in 1986.
One is seen on a local service in Edinburgh in the summer of 1987. The Lion never matched the success of the Citybus, managing just 32 sales.
Stewart J. Brown

Three coach-seated Lions were delivered to Eastern Scottish in 1987. They spent part of their lives in Scottish Citylink livery, providing high capacity on the busy Edinburgh–Glasgow corridor.
One unloads in Edinburgh bus station. All 19 Lions for the Scottish Bus Group had Alexander bodies.
Stewart J. Brown

Six Lions which had been built for Kelvin Scottish in 1986 entered service with Clydeside towards the end of 1987. They were painted in the company's Quicksilver livery, used for limited-stop services, in this case between Glasgow and Kilmacolm. A notice at the lower edge of the windscreen advises the driver that the vehicle is 14ft 9in high. This was a time when a standard-height double-decker was around 14ft 6in high, the added three inches on the Lion being one drawback of using a mid-mounted engine.
Stewart J. Brown

7 CHAPTER

New lives

Most buses enjoy a second life when they are retired by their original owners, but the upheavals of the late 1980s and early 1990s made for some interesting second lives for Ailsas and, to a lesser extent, Citybuses.

Among Ailsas, one of the earliest — and most surprising — moves was the purchase by London Buses in 1987 of 12 with Van Hool McArdle bodies from South Yorkshire PTE. They were operated by London Northern from Potters Bar garage, where they joined the three original trial Ailsas, which had migrated there at the end of 1986. They introduced a revised livery, with a black skirt and a band of white relief, NBC-style, between decks.

But an even bigger surprise came in the latter half of the year when London Buses bought the entire batch of 50 Alexander-bodied Ailsas from West Midlands Travel. These were shared between Potters Bar, which got 24, and Harrow Weald. The Ailsas at Harrow Weald were painted in the red and cream livery of Harrow Buses,

A significant number of South Yorkshire PTE's Van Hool McArdle-bodied Ailsas found new lives with unexpected buyers in 1986/7. London Buses took 12, one of which is seen in Enfield (above), while Eastern Scottish bought 25 for operation in Edinburgh. Neither operator had a history of buying second-hand buses in large numbers. Stewart J. Brown

while those at Potters Bar received the new black-skirted London Northern livery, as used on the ex-South Yorkshire buses. The Ailsas were 11 years old and with their noisy front-mounted 6.7-litre turbocharged engines were not universally popular with drivers used to more sophisticated rear-engined buses, although some valued their acceleration. They operated in London for just over three years. Most were withdrawn during 1990, the last coming out of service in January 1991.

South Yorkshire's Ailsas were also bought by two other major operators. Eastern Scottish took 25 in 1986 and operated them, primarily in Edinburgh, until 1990/1. Hampshire Bus also took a small number. One other London-area operator bought second-hand Ailsas for operation on LRT contracts — Boro'line Maidstone. In 1988 it bought eight 12-year-old Tayside buses with Alexander bodies for two Bexley-area services. Most were sold to Black Prince of Leeds in 1992.

All three of Greater Manchester's Ailsas were sold in 1990 to Lancaster City Transport, the newer pair moving on to Harris Bus of Grays in 1993, when Lancaster's operations were purchased by Stagecoach.

There was some movement of Ailsas within the Scottish Bus Group. The model was introduced to the Highland fleet in 1980, when Fife's first 10 were transferred north. They were at this time five years old. Eight of them went back to Fife in 1990. Highland also acquired one Ailsa from Midland, in 1981, and that too passed to Fife in 1990.

When SBG reorganised its subsidiaries in 1985 all 33 of Western's surviving Ailsas (one having been destroyed in an accident) passed to the new Clydeside company. In 1988 the nine oldest — 1978 buses — were transferred to Eastern, where in the same year they were joined by nine Central Ailsas; all were used mainly in the Edinburgh area. The new Strathtay company started life with five former Midland Ailsas, operating in Perth.

When Central and Kelvin were combined in 1989, the new Kelvin Central Buses operation took over the 20 remaining Ailsas in the Central fleet. The following year all eight Ailsas in the Midland fleet also joined KCB, to be followed by a few vehicles from Strathtay and from Fife.

In 1992 a fire at the Larkfield depot of Strathclyde Buses destroyed 60 buses and saw vehicles being hired in from other operators. These included 18 Ailsas from Tayside, which operated in Tayside livery but with their fronts painted in Strathclyde orange. Their centre exit doors were not used and were blocked by a metal panel which read, somewhat enigmatically, 'This is not a door'.

Although only one Ailsa was supplied new to an English independent, Premier of Stainforth in South Yorkshire, a significant number were bought second-hand by a colourful West Yorkshire business, Black Prince of Morley. During the 1990s Black Prince acquired Ailsas from a variety of sources, building up a fleet of nearly 40. These included vehicles which had been new to A1, Central SMT, Greater Glasgow, London Transport, Maidstone & District, South Yorkshire, Tayside, West Midlands and Western SMT. Oddities in the fleet were the Strathclyde single-deck rebuild and the dual-staircase London vehicle, which was acquired severely damaged and was restored over many years to its original condition.

Among the new generation of big bus groups First operated Ailsas in Glasgow and Edinburgh, including in Glasgow a few which survived long enough to gain corporate 'Barbie' livery. Citybuses were inherited by First from a number of companies including Badgerline, Strathclyde and Northampton. These were, of course, comparatively young buses when they were acquired, and many survived well into the 21st century.

Arriva almost avoided Ailsas — it acquired a few from Derby — but did operate large numbers of Citybuses, most notably the 88 bought new by Drawlane/British Bus and the 46 which had been in the Grey-Green fleet. Boro'line Maidstone's Citybuses also ended up with Arriva, via Kentish Bus, which had taken over Boro'line's London operations in 1992. Of the 36 H-registered Citybuses delivered to London & Country, 21 ended their days with Arriva's Midlands operations, some running in Derby alongside Citybuses bought new by Derby City Transport. Another 12 of London & Country's H-registered Citybuses moved north

Below: In December 1986 one of the West Midlands Ailsas suffered a major engine fire. The bus saw no further service with its original owner but was rebuilt by SBG Engineering and re-entered service with London Buses in March 1988. Adrian Pearson

at the same time (1998), six each going to Arriva Scotland West and to Arriva's operations in North West England.

Stagecoach acquired Ailsas and Citybuses from Fife, along with 12 almost-new Citybuses which had been delivered to Southdown, three of which soon migrated to Fife. Stagecoach sold all eight of Fife's 1984 Ailsas to Cardiff Bus in 1998/9.

After buying Citybuses in 1989 Trent decided to focus on single-deckers. When Trent withdrew its Citybuses in 1999/2000 — while they were still comparatively young — they

found ready buyers, 13 going to Plymouth Citybus, eight to Finglands in Manchester and the remaining three to two small operators — Burtons of Haverhill (two) and Reliance of Sutton-on-the-Forest.

In 2004 all 12 of Burnley & Pendle's 1988/9 Citybuses were bought by Lincolnshire Road Car, at that time still a subsidiary of Yorkshire Traction. They had been owned by Stagecoach when it ran the Burnley & Pendle business between 1997 and 2001 — and found their way back into the group when Stagecoach purchased Yorkshire Traction in 2005.

All 50 of the Ailsas delivered to West Midlands PTE in 1976 were purchased by London Buses in 1987. A London Northern example is seen in Enfield in 1990. Stewart J. Brown

London applied Harrow Buses livery to 26 of the West Midlands Ailsas. London Buses retained the electronic route-number display which had been fitted by the PTE when the buses were overhauled in 1984/5. Tony Wilson

Above: The Scottish Bus Group reorganisation of 1985 created a new Kelvin Scottish company, which in 1989 was combined with Central to form Kelvin Central Buses. KCB inherited Central's surviving Ailsas, initially painting them in a simplified version of Kelvin's blue and yellow livery (above left), and later in the red and cream (above right) which became the KCB standard. Both vehicles pictured are Mk II models from a batch of 20 delivered to Central in 1979. KCB used unusual blue and yellow destination blinds. Stewart J. Brown

Below: Strathtay Scottish, created in 1985 to combine parts of the Midland and Northern operations, acquired five Ailsas from Midland. The company adopted a distinctive livery, as demonstrated by this newly repainted bus in Perth in 1986. Stewart J. Brown

Black Prince of Leeds built up a sizeable fleet of Ailsas in the early 1990s, including 10 of the former West Midlands PTE vehicles which had spent time in London. Andrew Jarosz

There were three former South Yorkshire Ailsas in the Black Prince fleet, two of which wore green liveries to mark 21 years of operation in 1994. Andrew Jarosz

Tayside loaned 18 Ailsas to Strathclyde Buses in 1992 to cover a vehicle shortage caused by a major fire at Strathclyde's Larkfield garage. The front and rear of this bus have been repainted in Strathclyde orange. Stewart J. Brown

As well as buying new Citybuses Boro'line acquired eight 12-year-old Ailsas from Tayside in 1988 for operation on two LRT contracts in the Bexley area. These had dual-door Alexander bodywork. Note the LRT roundels placed on the blanked-off fog-lamp mouldings. These buses would be sold in 1992, most heading north to join the fleet of Black Prince in Leeds. Donald MacRae

In its early days FirstBus retained local identities. Only the 'f' logo alongside the SMT fleetname shows that this Ailsa in Edinburgh is operated by First. FirstBus predecessor GRT purchased the former Eastern Scottish business from its management in 1994.
Stewart J. Brown

FirstBus bought Strathclyde Buses in 1996 and for a short time traded as First Glasgow using a drab livery of unrelieved red, as seen here on one of the last batch of Ailsas for Strathclyde, delivered in 1984. Note the sliding cab door, which was a feature of later buses, and the passengers standing at the top of the stairs, highlighting the absence of seats at the front offside of the top deck.
Stewart J. Brown

A small number of Ailsas received First's corporate livery. This 2005 view in Glasgow's Great Western Road features a former Strathclyde PTE vehicle which by then was a creditable 21 years old — showing that some engineers' concerns about using a small turbocharged engine to power a double-deck bus were unfounded. *Billy Nicol*

Large numbers of Citybuses survived with First well into the 'Barbie' era. This bus had been new in 1990 to Northampton Transport but by 2005 had migrated north to join the First Edinburgh fleet. A number of ex-Northampton and ex-Strathclyde Citybuses survived in service with First Edinburgh in 2009, by which time the oldest had been in operation for 20 years. *Gavin Booth*

While part of Drawlane, four London & Country Citybuses with Northern Counties bodies were transferred to Bee Line Buzz in Manchester in 1992, when just three years old. They would later move to Midland Red North and would ultimately form part of the Arriva Midlands North fleet. Peter Rowlands

Derby City Transport was bought by British Bus, as Drawlane had become, in 1994. It adopted City Rider branding and a bright yellow, red and blue livery, as seen on this Marshall-bodied Citybus outside the city's bus station. Stewart J. Brown

Arriva inherited more than 150 Citybuses with the various businesses it absorbed, including 14 that had been new to North Western. These had East Lancs bodywork and included this example, seen in 1999 with branding for the Southport–Wigan service. Stewart J. Brown

Six single-door Alexander-bodied Citybuses that had been new to Grey-Green in 1990 were transferred in 1999 to Arriva Scotland West. Since 1990 Grey-Green had been owned by the Cowie group, which changed its name to Arriva in 1997, following its takeover of British Bus. Stewart J. Brown

Stagecoach acquired the Fife Scottish business in 1991 and with it what was left of a fleet of Ailsas, which had once numbered 74 vehicles. Its outsize fleetname largely obscured by advertising, a 1979 Mk II with Alexander body enters Kirkcaldy bus station.
Stewart J. Brown

Fife also operated Citybuses, and these too appeared in Stagecoach colours. One of 10 delivered in 1984 is seen 10 years later in Kirkcaldy.
The last Fife Citybuses were withdrawn from regular service in 2006.
Stewart J. Brown

Among the Citybuses operated by Stagecoach was the original East Lancs-bodied demonstrator of 1983, acquired with the A1 business in 1995.
Stewart J. Brown

Above: Stagecoach sold the newest of Fife's Ailsas, eight 1984 buses, to Cardiff Bus in 1998/9. The last of them survived in service in the Welsh capital until 2007. Stewart J. Brown

Below left: When Trent withdrew its Alexander-bodied Citybuses in 1999/2000 they found ready buyers, notably Plymouth Citybus, which purchased 13, one of which is seen here shortly after joining the Plymouth fleet. Mark Bailey

Below right: Later in their lives most of Plymouth's ex-Trent Citybuses were repainted yellow with Student Link branding and demoted to school-bus duties. The last of these were withdrawn in 2009. Mark Bailey

Appendices

1: SAMPLE SPECIFICATION COMPARISON

	1978 Ailsa	1984 Citybus
Wheelbase	4,953mm	4,953mm
Overall underframe length	9,781mm	9,514mm
Front overhang	2,400mm	2,263mm
Rear overhang	2,394mm	2,298mm
Frame height above front axle	743mm	787mm
Frame height above rear axle	740mm	800mm
Engine	TD70E	THD100EC
Cylinders	six	six
Capacity	6.7 litres	9.6 litres
Power output	193bhp @ 2,200rpm	210bhp @ 2,000rpm
Installed torque	660Nm @ 1,400rpm	830Nm @ 1,400rpm
Gearbox options	SCG Pneumocyclic	SCG Pneumocyclic
	Voith D851	Voith D851
	Allison MT640	ZF 4HP500
Suspension	leaf spring	air
Tyre size	11R 22.5	275/70R 22.5
Brake total friction area	4,494sq cm	6,865sq cm
Fuel tank capacity	250 litres	200 litres
Chassis weight	6,290kg	n/a
Complete vehicle unladen weight (Alexander body)	9,124kg	9,416kg
Maximum GVW	16,256kg	16,500kg

2: AILSA DELIVERIES IN THE UK, 1974-84

	1974	1975	1976	1977	1978	1979	1980	1981	1982	1983	1984	Total
Ailsa (demonstrator)	1											1
West Midlands PTE	3		50									53
Greater Glasgow PTE		18										18
Tyne & Wear PTE		3										3
West Yorkshire PTE		1										1
Alexander Fife		40		6		20					8	74
Maidstone & District		5										5
Tayside Regional Transport			35	17	3	21	35	15		35		161
A1 Service			3	2	3	3						11
South Yorkshire PTE			56	5	1							62
Premier, Stainforth			1									1
Derby Borough/City Transport				1					15			16
Alexander Midland				14								14
Eastern Scottish					10			20			10	40
Central SMT					10	20						30
Western SMT					10		24					34
Hanley Crouch Community Association					1							1
Greater Manchester PTE								1	2			3
Strathclyde PTE								40	41	35	15	131
Merseyside PTE									2		13	15
Cardiff City Transport									27	3	6	36
Volvo stock / Strathclyde PTE										1	2	3
London Buses											3	3
Total	**4**	**67**	**145**	**45**	**38**	**64**	**60**	**75**	**87**	**74**	**57**	**716**

3: CITYBUS DELIVERIES IN THE UK, 1982-93

	1982	1983	1984	1985	1986	1987	1988	1989	1990	1991	1992	1993	Total
Strathclyde	1		5					69	26				101
Derby City Transport		3	15		5		5						28
Nottingham City Transport		2		14			15	5					36 *
Volvo (demonstrators)	1			1		1							3
Tayside			5					15					20
Fife Scottish			2	10	21	2							35
Plymouth CityBus			2							2			4
A1 Service				2									2
London Buses				1									1
Eastern Scottish				5		4							9
Wright, Wrexham				1									1
Greater Manchester Buses					3					8	2		13
Bournemouth Transport					5		5	5					15
Northampton Transport					2			6	6	6	6	6	32
Great Yarmouth Transport						2		2					4
Western Scottish						4							4
Badgerline						12							12
Grey-Green						2	30		14				46
Boro'line Maidstone							1	14					15
Western National							3						3
Whippet, Hunstanton							1	2	1				4
Burnley & Pendle							2	10		3			15
Filer, Ilfracombe							1						1
Lincoln City Transport							4						4
Trent								24					24
Crawford, Neilston								1					1
Dewhirst, Bradford								1					1
Hanley Crouch Community Association								1					1
Finglands, Manchester								1					1
London & Country								38	21	15			74
London General								27	11	1			39
North Western								4	10				14
Southdown								12					12
Total	**1**	**6**	**29**	**34**	**36**	**27**	**67**	**237**	**89**	**35**	**8**	**6**	**575**

* Nottingham received a further 10 Citybuses in 1997 and one in 2002, taking the final UK total to 586.